CAMBRIDGE COMMONWEALTH SERIES

General Editor: Professor E. T. Stokes

The Durham Report and British Policy

CAMBRIDGE COMMONWEALTH SERIES

Toward 'Uhuru' in Tanzania: G. ANDREW MAGUIRE

Developing the Third World: The Experience of the Nineteen-Sixties:
RONALD ROBINSON (ed.)

These monographs are published by the Syndics of the
Cambridge University Press in association with the Managers of the
Cambridge University Smuts Memorial Fund for the advancement
of Commonwealth Studies

The Durham Report and British Policy

A Critical Essay

GED MARTIN

Research Fellow, Magdalene College, Cambridge

CAMBRIDGE at the University Press 1972

Published by the Syndics of the Cambridge University Press
Bentley House, 200 Euston Road, London NW1 2DB
American Branch: 32 East 57th Street, New York, N.Y. 10022

© Cambridge University Press 1972

Library of Congress Catalogue Card Number: 74-189596

ISBN: 0 521 08530 6

Printed in Great Britain by
W. Heffer & Sons Ltd, Cambridge

Contents

Preface

This book owes its origin to the History of the Commonwealth paper in Part II of the Cambridge Historical Tripos. I began teaching for this paper shortly after the start of a much larger research project of studying British policy towards British North America from 1837 to 1867. It was not long before I became aware of a gap between the books the undergraduates read about the Durham Report and what I was finding from my own work. There was a much greater awareness of Canadian problems in the late eighteen-thirties than was generally allowed, the extensive correspondence between Elgin and Grey at the time when responsible government was introduced into Canada was without a single reference to the Durham Report, and so on. At first, like many recent writers on the subject, I tried to moderate the extreme claims without attacking the main thesis that Durham was in some way a formative influence. This was an unsatisfactory compromise and I decided instead to discard the whole myth and start afresh. Once the preconceptions were shaken off, a very different picture appeared. The idea that Durham had been betrayed over the Bermuda ordinance quickly became untenable. Viewed through the eyes of contemporaries, including close friends and relatives, the Durham mission became a series of unpardonable disasters crowned by a departure unjustifiable both in itself and in the manner with which it was announced. Consequently Durham's contribution to the discussion of colonial policy was influential largely as an embarrassment. When I looked for the origin of Durham's fame as an Empire-builder I found that his reputation had revived too long after the event to make it possible to argue that it was an assessment of contemporaries, and too early to be claimed as the fruits of modern historical scholarship. In this I do not wish to slight the work of many imperial historians whom I greatly admire, but I do feel that the myth of the Durham Report is bound up with a constitutional approach to Commonwealth history, and that there is a case for attempting to interpret the subject from a different standpoint. I hope this book will be a contribution to that work of revision. Certainly my first thanks should go to all those who have studied the History of the Commonwealth at Cambridge and kept me continually aware of the problem.

My particular thanks are due to my friend Ronald Hyam for encouraging me to look at the subject from a new angle, and for his many suggestions particularly in the period of later imperial history which he knows so well. My thanks are also warmly given to Professor E. T. Stokes, general editor of the Commonwealth series, who first suggested this form of publication and has since aroused admiration for the patient way in which he has dealt with a particularly difficult author. I am also grateful to Professor Angus Ross of the University of Otago for his valuable comments, and to Dr J. R. Pole, my research supervisor, for his encouragement. I make no reference to my wife's services in deference to her wish that she should not be mentioned.

I owe thanks to the staffs of a large number of libraries and archives, especially to the University Library, Cambridge, the resources of which never fail to amaze me. All material from Crown-copyright records in the Public Record Office is published by permission of the Controller of the Stationery Office. I am grateful to have been able to use other manuscript collections listed in the bibliography, and my thanks are due to Mr Russell Ellice, Sir Fergus Graham and the Duke of Newcastle for permission to publish material from their family papers.

Ged Martin

Magdalene College
Cambridge
January 1972

The Durham Report and British Policy

A Critical Essay

1 THE PLACE OF THE REPORT IN COMMONWEALTH HISTORY

Historians of the British Empire have given the very highest praise to Lord Durham's *Report on the Affairs of British North America*, and its author has been regarded as the founder of the Commonwealth. 'Today he needs no vindication' wrote J. L. Morison in 1930 'for the later history of the British Empire has been the fulfilment of his dreams through obedience to his precepts.' To Sir Reginald Coupland, the Report 'became, to use a cant phrase, the Magna Carta of the Second British Empire'. As late as 1963 Gerald M. Craig could write that 'no attempt to debunk or deflate the great *Report* would be very successful'. For Professor Mansergh, the logical point at which to begin his fine survey of the *Commonwealth Experience* was Durham's ceremonial entry into Quebec, astride a white charger, at the outset of the mission which produced the Report.[1]

By no means all historians have gone to the lengths of Lucas, New and Coupland in their assessment.[2] 'To some extent the report has been overpraised', wrote E. L. Woodward in 1938, and here he echoed a reviewer of 1907.[3] But if many historians have tended to pitch their comments in a lower key, there can be no doubt that they have fundamentally accepted the verdict of Durham's most enthusiastic

---

[1] J. L. Morison, 'The Mission of the Earl of Durham' in *Cambridge History of the British Empire*, VI, pp. 289-307; R. Coupland, editor, *The Durham Report, an abridged version with an introduction and notes*, Oxford 1945, p. xlvi; G. M. Craig, editor, *Lord Durham's Report, An abridgement of the Report on the Affairs of British North America by Lord Durham*, Toronto 1963, p. i; P. N. S. Mansergh, *The Commonwealth Experience*, London 1969, pp. 30-41.

[2] C. P. Lucas, editor, *Lord Durham's Report on the Affairs of British North America* (3 vols.), Oxford 1912, esp. vol. I; Chester W. New, *Lord Durham: A Biography of John George Lambton First Earl of Durham*, Oxford 1929; R. Coupland, editor, *The Durham Report*, pp. xxviii-lxviii.

[3] E. L. Woodward, *The Age of Reform 1815-1870*, Oxford 1938, p. 365; *Review of Historical Publications relating to Canada*, XI, 1907, p. 91.

admirers. This can be seen in the treatment of the subject in three very different surveys of Commonwealth history written in the nineteen-sixties, those of W. D. McIntyre, R. A. Huttenback and Professor Mansergh.[4]

In some respects the task of the critic is made oddly difficult by the more moderate received view of the Report's significance. Many of the points made in this essay have been conceded long ago but − clear evidence of the extent to which historians have subscribed to the myth − the inferences and conclusions which should logically have been drawn from such concessions have never been made. Thus it has been accepted that the Report contained many inaccuracies, without re-alising that it cannot be maintained that it was a valuable source of information to the British public. It has been recognised that the Report was poorly received in England, but not appreciated that it is therefore difficult to argue that it was an influential document in re-lation to Canadian Union, although this may be because the extent of its poor reception among friend and foe alike has not been fully under-stood. If the criticisms of the Report and its place in imperial history which are offered here seem fierce, and on occasion to be attacking positions which by consensus historians would now regard as too extravagant to defend, it is because this moderate consensus is still one which rests upon an earlier assessment little short of hagiographical.

If the extreme view of the Report's significance is in some respects difficult to attack because of the muted tones in which it now appears, there are problems too for the critic in its full-blooded expression by New and Coupland. The problem is that the influence of the Report on subsequent events, such as Canadian Union or the introduction of responsible government, has been either assumed or argued on *post hoc ergo propter hoc* lines. A case which offers so little proof is peculiarly immune to conclusive disproof. In both the cases mentioned it would be impossible to maintain that the Report failed to exercise the slight-est influence even on a single individual. In short, however strong an assault is mounted, the traditional assessment of the Report can prob-ably never be destroyed, simply because it is based so extensively on

4 W. D. McIntyre, *Colonies into Commonwealth*, London 1966, pp. 46-8, 57; R. A. Huttenback, *The British Imperial Experience*, New York 1966, pp. 20-37; P. N. S. Mansergh, *The Commonwealth Experience*, pp. 30-41. An interesting recent comment on Durham is that of Peter Burroughs in his review of the 1969 reissue of New's biography. 'Our sober, detached appraisal of Durham's career has little in common with the emotional, patriotic involvement evinced by writers of a former generation when the British empire was in its heyday...' (*Canadian Historical Review*, LII, June 1971, pp. 190-1). The process of revision has tended to concentrate more on the extravagant presen-tation of the traditional view than upon that view itself.

assumption and so little on evidence. It is nonetheless the argument of this essay that the evidence shows the Report to have been remarkably uninfluential in Britain at the time of its publication, that it exercised little influence on British policy and that it owes its high position in imperial historiography mainly to later symbolic misconceptions, especially in the twentieth century.

One qualification must be made about the scope of this work. It examines the influence of the Durham Report in Britain and on British policy. This is a reasonable limitation, since in the mid nineteenth-century major policy decisions regarding the Empire were still by and large made in Britain. This is not to say that British decisions were not influenced by events in the colonies — indeed colonial realities frequently dictated a course which London could obstruct only to its own inconvenience.[5] But to accept this is not to accept that British policy was determined at one remove by the Durham Report. There is relatively little information about the reception of the Report around the Empire. In British North America it seems to have been the subject of lively discussion, mainly on party lines.[6] Sir Francis Head certainly feared that the circulation by the Reformers of a cheap edition of the Report was 'a poison which by day and by night is sickening unto death the loyalty of the Canadas'.[7] Head was perhaps a natural alarmist. A recent historian has stated that in Canada 'the note of criticism was loud and even strident'.[8] Outside British North America it is hard to measure the influence of the Durham Report. 'It has now gone the round, from Canada, through the West Indies and South Africa, to the Australasias, and has everywhere been received with acclamations,' wrote Wakefield in December 1839.[9] The *Colonial Gazette* said that 'in every colony where the English race has settled in considerable numbers, that document is a sort of political text-book'. The *Gazette* made it clear that the Report exercised a greater influence in the colonies than in Britain.[10] But how great or how lasting this influence was it is

---

5 Lord Durham's recommendation of responsible government arguably includes him among those who were prepared to let colonial reality dictate imperial policy. On the other hand, his wish to limit the extent of that self-government in the manner he proposed, his insistence on the anglicisation of French Canada, and his support for Wakefield's theories of settlement hardly support the claim.

6 Chester W. New, *Lord Durham*, pp. 528-43.

7 Public Archives of Canada, Derby Papers, microfilm A-30, 8, memorandum by F. B. Head, 62 Park St, Grosvenor Square, 25 May 1839.

8 G. M. Craig, editor, *Lord Durham's Report*, p. ix.

9 Wakefield to Durham, 26 December 1839, in Chester W. New, *op. cit.* p. 528.

10 *Colonial Gazette*, no. 90, 12 August 1840, p. 529 and see *ibid.* no. 88, 29 July 1840, p. 503.

hard to say. Only one point will be made here. It would be at least plausible to argue — even though it would not be true — that in Britain nothing was known about colonial self-government until the Durham Report provided for the first time an intelligent basis for discussion. But it would be utterly implausible to suggest that the ideas Durham put forward had never occurred to anyone in Australia or South Africa. That being so, the influence of the Report in the colonies would be limited mainly to its propaganda value, as Sir Francis Head feared, and the prestige which the support of an English earl gave to the Reformers. How valuable was the Report as a rallying cry and debating point cannot be said. Certainly one recent survey of the responsible government controversy in New South Wales is singularly sparse in its references to Durham.[11] The fact too that settler colonies advanced to self-government at very different speeds is a reminder that many other factors have to be taken into account. Thus while British policy was undoubtedly influenced by developments in the colonies, it would be still going beyond the evidence to assume from this that it was the Durham Report which provided 'the living force of the whole British Empire'.[12]

2   THE HISTORICAL CONTEXT OF THE DURHAM MISSION

To measure the significance of the Report it is necessary to place it in its proper context — of over twenty years of Canadian history; and of Durham's own mission to Canada. Too often the Report has been presented as a unique event in imperial history, or magnified out of proportion to its historical context, and it is not therefore surprising that it should have acquired an unwarranted importance. The problems of Lower Canada were not left unsolved because no one of Durham's vision has appeared to settle them, but because they were practically insoluble within the existing Empire. From 1819 onwards the French-dominated House of Assembly had attempted to make its grant of supply conditional on the control of all government expenditure, no

11   T. H. Irving, 'The Idea of Responsible Government in New South Wales before 1856', *Historical Studies Australia and New Zealand*, XI, 1963-5, pp. 192-205.

12   C. P. Lucas, editor, *Lord Durham's Report*, I, p. 316. In 1971 an article appeared which was strongly critical of the intolerant certainty which characterises most expressions of the Durham myth. The article, by Professor R. S. Neale, pointed to the existence of alternative proposals. Colonial self-government 'was probably the result of pressures within the colonies which were scarcely recognised let alone understood by Durham'. This is perhaps the most explicit criticism to come from the academic world. (R. S. Neale, 'Roebuck's Constitution and the Durham Proposals', *Historical Studies Australia and New Zealand*, XV, 1971, pp. 479-90.)

matter from what source the revenue had come. By 1827 relations between Governor Dalhousie and the Assembly hit rock-bottom. The Assembly refused to vote any money at all, and by way of reprimand it was dissolved. The radicals came back in even greater strength after the elections and Papineau, their leader, was elected Speaker. As in British Parliamentary practice, the formal consent of the Crown was requested to his election. Dalhousie refused to give it, and the Assembly retaliated by bringing constitutional government to a dead halt. A petition was sent to London, backed by 9,000 signatures and 78,000 crosses, and a Parliamentary Committee at Westminster examined the problem in 1828. It did not solve it, for the simple reason that the problem was insoluble.[1] By demanding control of expenditure, and an elective upper chamber, the French radicals were in effect asking for the creation of a second independent government in the Empire. This the British could not agree to in 1828, in 1839, or at any time down to 1846, because the Empire then formed a single tariff unit and therefore required a single executive. The real divide in imperial history is the ending of Protection in 1846, and the Durham Report, which is so often seen as the end of the imperial dark ages, is as much a product of them as any of the other deliberations on colonial policy before the eighteen-forties. The problem of Canada's position in the Empire failed to find a solution before the eighteen-forties, because the only possible solution — that of virtual independence — was not acceptable to the British until the introduction of Free Trade. It has often been argued that Durham was the first British statesman to express his faith in the possibility of a permanent connection between Britain and the colonies. This assertion is based mainly on a sentence from a letter written by Robert Baldwin to Durham,[2] and should in itself be regarded more as evidence that Durham was known to respond to flattery than as a definitive statement about British attitudes to Empire. All that can be said is that if the British were really so lukewarm about the connection, they showed a surprising determination to maintain a real measure of control over their most troublesome dependency. It is true that some, like Russell, foresaw a day when the colonies might be large enough and powerful enough to sever their links with Britain. But Durham too foresaw the same possibility, and was perhaps freer in his use of terms like 'colonial nationality' than many of his contemporaries. Both men in fact would have agreed with Roebuck, who told Howick of 'his strong preference of the connection between this country & Canada to its being joined to

---

[1] The Report of the 1828 Committee is in Parliamentary Papers, 1828, VII, 569, pp. 375-730.
[2] Robert Baldwin to Durham, 23 August 1838, in Arthur G. Doughty, *Report of the Public Archives for the Year 1923*, Ottawa 1924, pp. 326-7.

the United States'.[3] The British, then, were not lukewarm about their colonies, and precisely for that reason they had not 'solved' the problem of Lower Canada.[4]

That the problem of Lower Canada could not be solved within the framework of a mercantilist empire was underlined by the failure of the Howick Act of 1831. The Act was a bold and optimistic attempt at compromise, worthy of the vision of Lord Howick, the Under-Secretary for Colonies largely responsible for it. The Assembly's claim for control of expenditure was conceded, in exchange for a reserved Civil List of £19,500, designed to ensure the continuation of at least some form of government under all circumstances. The Act reflected the Whig belief in the ability of compromise to reconcile opposites, and their faith in human nature — if you go half-way to meet your opponent, he will come half-way to meet you. Regrettably it soon appeared that Papineau was not a Whig. Far from being appeased by the Howick Act, he moved further towards extremism. He broke first with John Neilson, leader of the English-speaking liberals of Lower Canada, and then quarrelled with the Catholic Church. The Orleanist revolution in 1830, the cholera of 1832, and the violent by-election in Montreal the same year all increased the pace of French nationalism. The control of supply given by the Howick Act as a gesture of generous compromise, was used year by year to cut off all revenue to the colonial government.[5] 'The truth is Howick led us into a Scrape,' wrote one ex-Whig to another in 1838. Significantly the letter continued, 'Will Durham get us out of it?'[6]

Thus by the middle of the eighteen-thirties Canada provided the Whigs with a problem which was not simply practical but theoretical too. The great Whig administration of 1830 was running out of steam. Essentially the Whigs were very conservative reformers. Even Howick and Durham, who were close to the radicals, were both firm supporters of the Established Church. Whig reform was intended to save, and not destroy the existing order — expressed in Russell's verdict of 'finality'. But paradoxically the Government which set out to make the world

---

3 University of Durham, Grey Papers, Journal of 3rd Earl Grey, C3/3, 29 December 1837.

4 Peter Burroughs has dismissed the idea that British statesmen were indifferent to the colonial connection as 'factually untrue' (*Canadian Historical Review*, LII, June 1971, pp. 190-1). Compare this with *Review of Historical Publications relating to Canada*, XI, 1907, p. 90. 'In 1837 the Whig leaders wished, if they decently could, to break the political tie with Canada. . .'

5 This sketch of political developments in Lower Canada is based on C. E. Fryer, 'Lower Canada (1815-1837)' in *Cambridge History of the British Empire*, VI, pp. 234-50.

6 University Library, Cambridge, Graham Papers (microfilm no. 30) Bundle 35, Graham to Stanley, private, Netherby, 21 January 1838.

safe for Whiggery had unintentionally revealed a world which was neither to its liking nor within its comprehension. In Ireland Whiggery was proving inadequate, in Canada it was at best irrelevant, at worst, as in the failure of the Howick Act, completely counter-productive. They were brought face to face with the unpleasant fact that the kind of solution applicable to Canada was too dangerous in its implications for Britain. In 1836, for instance, they had contemplated the abolition of the Legislative Council in Lower Canada, in order to circumvent Papineau's demands to have it made elective. William IV objected violently, saying that it would lead to the abolition of the House of Lords, and threatened to have Melbourne impeached if he went any further.[7] The King was to say the least eccentric, but there was little doubt that others would have raised the same objection, and no such measure would have passed the Lords. Roebuck, the spokesman in Parliament for the Assembly of Lower Canada, regretted that the question of the Canadian upper house had arisen 'at an inopportune moment when we ourselves are discussing the merits of our own House of Lords'. Roebuck, however, thought the Lords did themselves little honour by supposing that their fate must be determined by that of the unpopular Legislative Council of Lower Canada.[8] Unable then to take action on the scale that could have broken the deadlock, the Whigs could only drift along with an insoluble problem. When Normanby handed over the seals of the Colonial Office to Russell in 1839 he explained that the real art of governing the colonies was to decide which problems needed immediate solution and 'which might by post-ponement dispose of themselves — a process to which you will find after a little practise (*sic*) many Colonial questions are not unapt to yield'.[9] Bankruptcy of dogma made this into Whig policy.

So too did tactical necessity. The General Elections of 1835 and 1837 left the Whigs heavily dependent upon the well-organised Irish and the unorganised radicals. For religious and political reasons both groups were sympathetic to the French Canadians, and the need to hold their support was a further reason for cautious inactivity on the part of the Government. Whig dependence on the O'Connellites was underlined at the start of the 1838 session of Parliament, when Peel was able successfully to challenge the preamble to Durham's instructions because

---

[7] Lord Broughton, *Recollections of a Long Life* (6 vols.), London 1909-11, V, pp. 41-2.

[8] *Hansard's Parliamentary Debates*, 3rd series, XXXVII, 14 April 1837, cols. 1209-29.

[9] Public Record Office, Russell Papers, PRO 30/22/3D. Normanby to Russell, n.p., n.d. (22 September 1839), fos. 1280-7. This letter appears to be a copy of a less legible letter at fos. 1245-52.

the Holyhead coach was late in delivering the Irish members.[10] The radicals mattered less as a group because they were less compact, but they became increasingly dissatisfied with the Government over Canada. The principal importance of the radical viewpoint was that it was shared by Lord Howick. The eldest son of Earl Grey, Howick sat in the Commons where he and Russell were the only real men of business on the Whig front bench. (It was their joint threat of resignation in February 1839 which obliged Melbourne to dismiss Glenelg from the Colonial Office — a fall which had nothing to do with the Durham Report, as alleged by Wakefield.)[11] Howick was not himself a radical so much as an advanced Whig — he ended his long life a Conservative, in perfect fidelity to his fixed beliefs: dislike of democracy, disestablishment and Gladstone. But he seemed more radical than perhaps he was, and certainly he had long felt that there was 'a real difference of opin^n on colonial politics (*sic*) between me & the majority of the cabinet'. An attack by the radical MP Warburton on the Government's handling of the Canada question was so close to his own opinions that it 'made me feel very uncomfortable'. Fundamentally Howick was a sensitive man, who hid his emotions behind an abrupt and sometimes brutal manner. He was a difficult Cabinet colleague, apt to threaten resignation if he failed to get his way. Yet a Government as weak in personnel as Melbourne's could not afford to lose a man of such ability. When rebellion broke out in Canada, when force finally became unavoidable, Howick was still bitterly insisting that repression must be combined with conciliation, and it was largely to appease him that Durham was sent to Canada.[12]

---

10 *The Times*, 26 January 1838.

11 Wakefield to Durham, n.d., quoted in Chester W. New, *op. cit.* p. 493. In fact Glenelg was dismissed after an ultimatum from Howick and Russell, and the immediate cause of their concern was Glenelg's handling of the Jamaica problem. Certainly neither man referred to the impending appearance of the Durham Report, although New attempts to bolster Wakefield's unfounded claim with the statement that among the ministers Howick and Russell 'were presumably the most favourable to Durham. . .' (University of Durham, Grey Papers, Russell to Howick, confidential, Wilton Crescent, 31 January 1839, and Journal of 3rd Earl Grey, C3/4, 2 February 1839 *et seq., Chester W. New, op. cit.* p. 393). This is one small example of the process of *post hoc ergo propter hoc* reasoning which has been employed to establish a causal connection between the Durham Report and subsequent events in imperial history. For Glenelg's resignation, see Edith Dobie, 'The Dismissal of Lord Glenelg from the office of Colonial Secretary', *Canadian Historical Review*, XXIII, 1942, pp. 280-5.

12 William Carr, 'Henry George Grey, Third Earl Grey', *Dictionary of National Biography*, Supplement II, pp. 361-4; University of Durham, Grey Papers, Journal of 3rd Earl Grey, C3/4, 2 February 1839; *ibid.* C3/3, 22 December 1837; Lord Esher, editor, *The Girlhood of Queen Victoria. A Selection from*

But this is looking ahead a little. In 1835 the Whigs simply did not know what to do about Canada, and even if they had, they lacked the power to do it. So they did what any other set of politicians would have done in the same position. They appointed a Royal Commission, headed by the Earl of Gosford, and hoped that the problem would by postponement dispose of itself. The appointment of a Royal Commission was of course a device used very successfully by the Whigs in their programme of domestic reform. The Gosford Commission however was set to solve a problem already almost beyond reach of legislation, and not surprisingly it failed to agree on any significant course of action. It is difficult to escape the belief that its appointment was at least partly a product of desperation. *The Times* was to condemn it as 'a frivolous and toad-eating embassy'. 'Every honest man declared that it was a temporizing mission, a bribe to the Radicals in the British Parliament to tolerate the Whig Ministry . . .'[13] Howick recalled that he had opposed the creation of the Commission 'on the ground that we were then as well aware as we could be after receiving their Reports' of what was wrong in Canada. To Howick the Gosford Commission was 'merely a device for postponing any decision on the policy to be adopted'.[14] But the Commissioners did their work carefully and conscientiously. Sir Charles Grey, who frequently disagreed with his colleagues Sir George Gipps and Gosford, produced a plan for dividing Lower Canada into a federation of five units — arranged to give an English majority.[15] This was taken up in the Colonial Office, and produced a round-about revival of the scheme for union of the. Provinces attempted in 1822, since provision could be made for Upper Canada eventually to become the sixth unit in the federation.[16] But

Her Majesty's Diaries between the years 1832 and 1840 (2 vols.), London 1912, I, pp. 263-4 (25 January 1838), pp. 251-2 (4 January 1838); Howick to Melbourne, private, Holland House, 29 December 1837 in Lloyd C. Sanders, editor, *Lord Melbourne's Papers*, London 1889, pp. 423-4; Public Record Office, Russell Papers, PRO 30/22/3A, Howick to Russell, private, Whitehall Place, 1 January 1838, fos. 1-2, and his Paper on Canada, fos. 18-29, of which original drafts, dated 29 December 1837, are in University of Durham, Grey Papers, Colonial Papers 100-1.

13 *The Times*, 23 December 1837.
14 Public Record Office, Russell Papers, PRO 30/22/2B, 'Memorandum on the Affairs of Canada drawn up & read to the Cabinet May 30th 1836', fos. 490-502.
15 Parliamentary Papers 1837, XXIV, 50, pp. 1-408, esp. pp. 246-8, for Sir Charles Grey's minute of 17 November 1836.
16 Public Record Office, CO 537/137, Supplementary Correspondence, British North America 1834-60. Minute by James Stephen, Secret, Colonial Office, 20 December 1836, fos. 144-69 and copy fos. 170-95, which led to 'Epitome of a Proposed Canada Act', confidential, Colonial Office, 19 January 1837, fos. 196-202, and an undated 'Heads of a Bill for the Better Government of Upper Canada and Lower Canada', confidential, fos. 204-8.

overall the Gosford Commission failed to come up with any startling or novel solution. Nor was this to be wondered at. T. F. Elliot, Secretary to the Commission, wrote privately to dampen Howick's optimism. Papineau, in Elliot's opinion, had chosen to make an issue of the composition of the Legislative Council precisely because it was a non-resolvable grievance. 'Negotiation with Papineau appears to me to be hopeless'.[17] Certainly one of the most convincing arguments which was later to be urged for responsible government was that an Assembly with real power would never have fallen under the sway of so negative an agitator.[18] But the predictable failure of the Gosford Commission to break out of the political deadlock should not cause it to be written off altogether. It delivered a whole series of informative reports, adding to the mass of evidence previously published by the Committee of 1828. It investigated the Crown lands, the claims of the Assembly, responsible government, the Legislative Council, the vexed question of the lands of the Seminary of Montreal, as well as miscellaneous complaints. These were questions which were to be considered in the Durham Report, based on a much briefer mission than that of the Gosford Commissioners, and acknowledged by its admirers to be inaccurate and misleading in many places. Yet one of the major claims made on behalf of the Durham Report is that it was a valuable descriptive work. 'For the British Government and people at the time, woefully ignorant in regard to Canada, its informative value far outweighed its misleading features'.[19] Even if the internal inconsistency of this statement is overlooked — how were the British to know which parts were misleading? — it is a view which can only be sustained by divorcing the Report from its context of previous official reports, pamphlets, articles and editorials. Many people were indeed ignorant about Canada, but their ignorance was not caused by lack of official and unofficial information about the subject. Certainly the failure of politicians to solve its problems was not the result of ignorance on their part. The Durham Report was unquestionably livelier than the Gosford Report, but this did not necessarily make it more reliable or influential. Indeed, Russell broadly hinted that its comments on the French Canadians were not simply lively but lurid.[20] But whatever the merits or demerits of the presen-

---

17 University of Durham, Grey Papers, Elliot to Howick, Montreal, 18 July 1836, in answer to Howick to Elliot (copy), private, War Office, 19 May 1836.
18 E.g. by Joseph Howe in his 'Letters to Lord John Russell' in H. E. Egerton and W. L. Grant, *Canadian Constitutional Development shown by selected speeches and despatches, with introductions and explanatory notes*, London 1907, pp. 190-252, esp. p. 245.
19 Chester W. New, *op. cit.* p. 496.
20 *Hansard's Parliamentary Debates*, 3rd series, XLVII, 3 June 1839, cols. 1254-75.

tation, the Durham Report cannot fairly be claimed to have unleashed a flood of new information on the country. At least one reviewer claimed to be unable to understand why it had been necessary to mount an expensive transatlantic mission to enable Durham to discover what everyone else had already read in the published record. Another felt that Canada might have been spared the whole episode had Durham been locked up in London with 'a decent Gazeteer, Montgomery Martin's History of the Colonies, and an edition of Mr. Roebuck's speeches'.[21]

The failure of the Gosford Commission to produce an acceptable overall solution for Canada was rapidly followed by a deterioration of an already bad situation. Russell's ten resolutions of March 1837[22] weakened the Government by offending the radicals, and raised tempers to dangerous levels in Lower Canada. Finally in November 1837 an ill-advised attempt to arrest Papineau sparked off a rebellion among the French, and a largely emulatory outbreak followed in Upper Canada. In an age of slow communications the news did not reach London until 22 December.[23] For the Whigs it was to be a miserable Christmas.

For the imperial historian, the main question which arises in response to the rebellion is, what did the Whigs decide to do about Canada? To this the traditional answer is that they appointed Durham early in 1838, received his Report in 1839 and acted on part of it in 1840. In itself it is implausible that such a conscious and intended series of actions should be attributed to the Melbourne government, which in fact drifted without any clear *raison d'être* from one crisis to the next, on little more than a week to week basis. But the real problem is that historians have asked the wrong question about the Whig response to the rebellions. They were indeed concerned about Canada, but Canada was nearly three weeks' sail away. Whether the rebellion would succeed or fail, its outcome had probably been decided already. They could, and did, send off reinforcements – which Russell was later to admit they should have done long before.[24] But even so, there was little they could do at that distance of time and space to influence the crisis in Canada. The immediate concern of the Melbourne Government, then,

---

21 *Dublin University Magazine*, LXXV, March 1839, p. 355; *Canadian, British American, and West Indian Magazine*, I, March 1839, p. 62. Robert Montgomery Martin produced an endless series of books on the colonies, most of which were badly digested abridgements of official Reports.

22 The resolutions are given in Parliamentary Papers, 1837, XLII, O. 42, pp. 1-4.

23 University of Durham, Grey Papers, Journal of 3rd Earl Grey, C3/3, 22 December 1837; *The Times*, 23 December 1837.

24 University of Durham, Grey Papers, Russell to Grey, n.p., 12 March 1848.

was not to save Canada but to save themselves. It was no surprise that revolt had broken out in Canada, and both the Tories and the Radicals were all too likely to launch fierce Parliamentary assaults, the one group asserting that the Whigs had been too lenient, the other that they had been too harsh. Indeed, it was really Peel's honourable refusal to join forces with the Radicals on this flimsy basis which was to save the Melbourne Government.[25] But the Government could not rely entirely on the forbearance of their opponents, and badly needed to regain the political initiative in Britain by some move of its own. Its first response was to announce that Parliament would be recalled from its Christmas recess a fortnight earlier than usual.[26] This was, and remains, a traditional response to political crisis in Britain, and is designed to show that the Government views the particular situation seriously and therefore by implication to give the impression that it is in control. The announcement of an early recall of Parliament could have no effect on immediate events in Canada, but was solely designed to recapture the initiative in British politics. At the same time, bringing forward the meeting of Parliament by a fortnight gave the Ministers a fortnight less to come up with a plausible plan with which to confound their opponents. It is scarcely surprising that they turned to the idea of sending out a strong man in the hope that he would settle Canada's problems on the spot.

The strong man chosen was the Earl of Durham, and he was chosen less for his own merits than from the need to conciliate Lord Howick. Obviously in the aftermath of revolt the old constitution would have to be suspended. But Howick doggedly insisted that repression by itself would only worsen the situation.[27] 'Many of my colleagues', wrote Melbourne to Durham, 'would not be induced to concur in giving such powers unless to a person, like yourself, of great personal weight and of

---

25 See Gladstone's memorandum of Peel's remarks at a meeting of Conservative leaders, 20 January 1838, in John Morley, *Life of William Ewart Gladstone* (3 vols.), London 1903, I, pp. 641-2.

26 The decision to recall Parliament early was literally the first response made to the news by a group of senior ministers, and was announced that evening to the Commons by Russell. University of Durham, Grey Papers, Journal of 3rd Earl Grey, C3/3, 22 December 1837, and *Hansard's Parliamentary Debates*, 3rd series, XXXIX, 22 December 1837, cols. 1428-31.

27 Public Record Office, Russell Papers, PRO 30/22/3A, Howick to Russell, private, Whitehall, 1 January 1838, fos. 1-2. Durham did not sympathise with Howick's opposition to the suspension of the constitution, 'for how can he call into Existence a House of Assembly the members of which are now actually in arms against the Government of the Mother Country?' (National Library of Scotland, Ellice Papers, E30, Durham to Ellice, London, 1 January 1838, fos. 45-6.)

known popular and liberal principles.'[28] Months later, when much had happened to make the Ministers regret their appointment, Russell still felt that only with Durham as Governor-General would 'our friends' have accepted the despotic rule which the situation in Canada had necessitated.[29] It was this which contributed to Durham's own bitterness: 'I undertook the office after two refusals, as a favor conferred on *them. I* did not want it. I abominated it. But I was told their Existence as a Gov^t depended on their being able to shew a prospect of settling the Canadian Question. I sacrificed myself to save them & how have I been repaid?'[30] Durham had first been asked to go to Canada in the summer of 1837, but at that time he had decided to 'have nothing to do with the settlement of that unfortunate question'.[31] The idea of sending Durham to Canada had come from Howick. In opposing the creation of the Gosford Commission Howick had preferred a plan of 'giving extensive powers to one Individual as Governor'[32] and the failure of the Commission encouraged him to press again for a Governor-General with real, not nominal, power over the whole of British North America, and 'the most extensive powers with respect to the terms to be given to the Canadians'. Durham's 'standing in the political world w^d be sufficient justification for the extraordinary powers committed to him'. Howick believed that since the Colonial Office under Glenelg would never get round to sending out firm instructions, it was necessary to find a man who was capable of acting on his own initiative. He believed Durham was such a man, and hoped that he would see it as a way of winning 'the strongest claims' to high office on his return. Furthermore, Howick remained optimistic that Durham would eventually accept, attributing his refusal in August 1837 to Melbourne's failure to ask him properly.[33] Consequently, when the rebellion broke out and Howick was on the verge of resignation, it was

[28] Melbourne to Durham, Windsor Castle, 7 January 1838, in Stuart J. Reid, *Life and Letters of the First Earl of Durham, 1792-1840* (2 vols.), London 1906, II, pp. 148-9.

[29] Public Record Office, Russell Papers, PRO 30/22/3B, Russell to Melbourne (copy), Brighton, 25 October (1838), fos. 736-9.

[30] National Library of Scotland, Ellice Papers, E30, Durham to Ellice, private, Cleveland Row, 26 December 1838, fos. 70-3.

[31] Melbourne to Durham, 22 July 1837, in Stuart J. Reid, *First Earl of Durham*, II, pp. 137-9; National Library of Scotland, Ellice Papers, E30, Durham to Ellice, confidential, Lambton Castle, 27 August 1837, fos. 37-8.

[32] Public Record Office, Russell Papers, PRO 30/22/2B, 'Memorandum on the Affairs of Canada drawn up & read to the Cabinet May 30th 1836' (by Howick), fos. 490-502.

[33] National Library of Scotland, Ellice Papers, E22, Howick to Ellice, private, Glasgow, 22 August 1837, fos. 27-8.

necessary to renew the invitation to Durham to keep the Government together. Durham himself was not sympathetic to his brother-in-law's objections, sardonically predicting that the ministers would have to choose between Howick and Canada.[34] But leading Whigs were well aware of the need to 'satisfy Howick' and Durham himself helped to dissuade him from resigning.[35]

One point was clear in January 1838. Durham was appointed to govern Canada, not to write a report about it. 'Further enquiry after the miserable abuse of this pretext for delay by Glenelg's commission w^d be justly scouted by all parties in the House of Commons.'[36] The report only arose out of the failure of the mission.

The argument that Durham was 'of known popular and liberal principles' and might somehow succeed in mollifying the Canadians, was just plausible enough to ward off opposition attacks. The *Examiner*, a radical weekly, noted that the Tory press was 'puzzled' by his appointment, 'not knowing how to disapprove, yet shrinking back from honest approval'. A typical comment was that of *The Times*. 'We sincerely wish Lord Durham success in his mission: we certainly do not venture to predict it.'[37] At both extremes of politics there were those who felt that Durham had been offered the job to get him out of the country, and there is probably an element of truth in this.[38] Certainly when it began to appear that he would throw up his task in the autumn of 1838, the first reaction of senior ministers was to consider offering him the Lord Lieutenancy of Ireland.[39] But while the prospect of Durham hundreds of miles away may have appealed to some of its members, for the Government as a whole the appointment was a short-term political expedient. At one and the same time it enabled the Government to regain the initiative when Parliament reassembled, to make it difficult for the Opposition to attack their failings without appearing to be unpatriotically undermining the authority of the Queen's represen-

---

[34] For Howick's resignation threat, see National Library of Scotland, Ellice Papers, E22, Howick to Ellice, private, W.O. (4 January 1838), fos. 29-32; *ibid.* E30, Durham to Ellice, private, Cleveland Row, 30 December 1837, fos. 41-2.

[35] Public Record Office, Russell Papers, PRO 30/22/3A, Memorandum by Ellice, Holkham, 7 January 1838, fos. 40-2; National Library of Scotland, Ellice Papers, E30, Durham to Ellice, private, London, 1 January 1838, fos. 45-6.

[36] National Library of Scotland, Ellice Papers, E22, Howick to Ellice, private, W.O. (4 January 1838), fos. 29-32.

[37] *Examiner*, no. 1565, 28 January 1838, p. 59; *The Times*, 17 January 1838.

[38] E.g. *The Times*, 7 April 1838; *Spectator*, no. 555, 16 February 1839, pp. 155-6.

[39] Public Record Office, Russell Papers, PRO 30/22/3B, Russell to Melbourne (copy), Brighton, Oct. 18, 5 o'clock (1838), fos. 715-16.

tative, while postponing for just a little longer the vexed question of what to do with Lower Canada.[40]

It may be objected that this interpretation is unfair to the Whigs, crediting them with no public spirit and attributing to them a cynical desire to keep office more fitting to politicians of the mid-twentieth century. There is, however, no reason to suppose that the human nature of politicians was any different in the eighteen-thirties than it is now, and it would be naïve to consider the measures taken in a crisis by a weak government without examining the effects on that government's strength. In one important respect, the behaviour of the Whigs is more characteristic of the early Victorian period than it would have been later. Unlike the governments of the late nineteenth century and after, Melbourne's could not count on the support of a disciplined party. With a small majority it was peculiarly vulnerable to defections which it might have defied in the age of the well-whipped caucus. Colonial issues were certainly regarded as fair game for party attack. Eighteen months after Durham's appointment, the Whigs were briefly turned out of office after defeat on a West Indian issue. Peel's comment was, 'Jamaica was a good horse to start'.[41] Melbourne gave a clear idea of his own priorities in his letter to Durham in July 1837. 'The final separation of those colonies might possibly not be of material detriment to the interests of the Mother Country, but it is clear that it would be a serious blow to the honour of Great Britain, and certainly would be fatal to the character and existence of the Administration under which it took place.'[42]

But Durham's appointment was not to remain a valuable expedient for very long, even by the limited horizons of the Melbourne government. The reasons for the failure of the mission are to be sought in the personality of Durham himself. Subsequent generations have tended to think not so much of Durham the man as of Durham the author of a much praised Report. But it is worth remembering that when the Report appeared in 1839 the emphasis was reversed and to contemporaries it was something written by, and overshadowed by, Durham himself. To subsequent generations Durham takes colour from his Report. In 1839 it was the other way round, and Durham was far from being a widely loved figure. Despite his jolly nickname, 'Radical Jack' was nobody's pet. Melbourne confessed that he could not understand

40 Perhaps mention should be made of one small cloud which appeared when the appointment was announced. The *Sun*, itself a liberal paper, asked, 'Why was Lord Brougham overlooked?' (*Sun*, 17 January 1838).

41 John Morley, *Life of William Ewart Gladstone*, I, p. 222.

42 Melbourne to Durham, 22 July 1837 in Stuart J. Reid, *op. cit.* II, pp. 137-9.

why men feared Durham so much.[43] But fear him they did. The roots of his explosive personality lay in a lonely childhood, and in particular the lack of a father who might have channelled his strong character away from the displays of petulant vanity and attention seeking which were to mark so much of his public career.[44] To contemporaries, however, particularly if they were the victims of Durham's behaviour, charitable psychological explanations were too much to accept. Durham displayed a critically dangerous mixture of radicalism and vanity, and many a respectable English gentleman must have seen in him an alarming echo of revolutionary France. 'Haughty, petulant, and self-willed, yet yielding with more than woman's weakness to the flatterer's arts, vain to excess of newly-acquired aristocratic honours, yet as avaricious of mob popularity as if he were a democrat at heart' – thus wrote an arch-Tory paper on the man whose twin aims in 1831 had been suffrage for the masses and an earldom for John George Lambton.[45] Mid-twentieth century Britain has been served by a whole series of men, neutral in their public politics, who have undertaken official enquiries and produced neutral, sometimes radical reports – men such as Lord Hunt, Lord Redcliffe-Maud, Mr Justice Milner-Holland, Lord Devlin and Lord Pearson. Durham was not one of these. He descended from no position of lofty political neutrality to recommend an impartial policy for Canada. He was known to be an extremist both in politics and personal behaviour, and it was as the work of an extremist that his Report was received.

In the context of official reports of the time, which were often frankly propagandist, this point may seem too obvious to be stated. But in the context of imperial history, in which the Durham Report and the Balfour Report of 1926 are sometimes linked together as joint pillars of the Commonwealth,[46] it is worth pointing out that while the latter was the work of a respected elder statesman, the former was written by a controversial radical.

---

[43] Melbourne to Russell, South Street, 31 October 1838, in Lloyd C. Sanders, editor, *Lord Melbourne's Papers*, pp. 434-5.

[44] Chester W. New, *op. cit.* p. 4. 'He was a spoiled child as fatherless boys are apt to be, and throughout his life his spirit bore the marks of that experience. From the first his temperament – imperious, impulsive, extremely sensitive – was a difficult one to deal with.' Durham himself confessed to Lord Grey 'I have never felt the blessing of a father's care or advice and, I fear, I have suffered much for it. . .', and it is clear that he looked to his father-in-law to supply the deficiency. (Durham to Grey, 11 December 1816, in *ibid.* pp. 16-17.)

[45] *Morning Herald*, 20 October 1838.

[46] E.g. V. Halperin, *Lord Milner and the Empire. The Evolution of British Imperialism*, London 1952, p. 222.

Between 1832 and 1837 Durham had undertaken two missions to St Petersburg, and it was this experience — combined with his position in British politics — which gave him sufficient stature to be a plausible choice as High Commissioner in Canada. Cynics suggested that his principal qualification for the post was that he had spent two winters in a cold climate.[47] But the missions to Russia had revealed some of the weaknesses of Durham's character, and these soon began to be probed by the Tory press. The Tsar, it was pointed out, had refused to accept Stratford Canning as British ambassador in 1833, but had got on very well with Durham.[48] The Tsar had showered Radical Jack with Russian decorations — many considered it unfitting that a British nobleman should be so proud of the awards of a foreign sovereign — and Durham in his turn forgot all about the sufferings of Poland. Indeed, in Poland as in Canada, he was to show a remarkable lack of sympathy for the claims of 'small nations struggling to be free'.[49]

The implications of the Russian experience were none too subtly hammered out: Durham was so dazzled by the display of power that he lost sight of Britain's true interests. To the nickname 'Dictator', *The Times* pointedly added 'the Czar of all the Canadas'. Durham, it claimed, was 'irritable and arbitrary' and 'open as a schoolgirl to skilful flattery'.[50] The evidence of the press cannot be taken as the impartial judgement of disinterested observers — least of all that of *The Times*. All the same, their picture of Durham does not differ greatly from that offered by two such sympathetic biographers as Reid and New. His contemporary enemies did not however seek the excuses for his conduct which have been presented by his subsequent admirers.[51] Whether the picture was true or not, a large section of the public believed that vanity was Durham's crucial weakness, and errors of judgement he was

---

47 The remark was attributed to Brougham by *Canadian, British American and West Indian Magazine*, I, March 1839, p. 68.

48 As Lord Stratford de Redcliffe, Canning was to have his revenge in the Crimean War.

49 *The Times*, 7 April 1838; *Canadian, British American and West Indian Magazine*, I, March 1839, pp. 58, 64. (At p. 58 the writer regretted that 'unhappy Poland had no grand crosses to bestow, and no Imperial palaces to feast in'.) Englishmen did not, of course, see Poland and French Canada in the same light, although Roebuck attempted to draw the comparison. (*Spectator*, no. 542, 17 November 1838, pp. 1084-5, his letter of 15 November.)

50 *The Times*, 7 August 1838; 18 January 1838.

51 Reid's biography was criticised for its 'undiscriminating hero-worship' by H. E. Egerton in England, and the same criticism was voiced in Canada. Even Chester New was gently chided for the same offence, and in his own country (*English Historical Review*, XXII, 1907, pp. 187-8; *Review of Historical Publications relating to Canada*, XI, 1907, pp. 89-92; *Canadian Historical Review*, XI, 1930, pp. 49-53).

to commit under the strain of ill-health were to be interpreted as petulance.[52]

Durham landed in Canada on 29 May 1838 and left on 1 November of the same year. His mission had collapsed about him even before that, largely because of what seemed merely a legal technicality. After the rout of the rebellion, most of its leaders succeeded in escaping to the U.S.A. A few fell into the hands of the Government, and when Durham arrived in Lower Canada a group of eight prisoners constituted a particular problem.[53] Trial by jury in the truculent atmosphere of Lower Canada would almost certainly have led to their acquittal in the teeth of the evidence, although all eight acknowledged their guilt. Yet it was essential that the ring-leaders should receive exemplary punishment, in order that an amnesty might be extended to the rank and file without appearance of weakness. It was certainly to Durham's personal credit that he did not attempt to pack a jury to secure a verdict of guilty. But this does not mean that his solution was necessarily better. After some curious unofficial bargaining with the accused, Durham issued an ordinance banishing them to Bermuda on pain of execution if they ever returned to Canada.[54] In England, Brougham pounced on the Ordinance.[55] Durham's authority did not extend to Bermuda, and disquiet was felt at even the conditional infliction of the death penalty without trial. The Government wavered, attempted to defend Durham, but finally on 10 August Melbourne announced that the Ordinance would be disallowed.[56] When Durham heard of this he resigned his post in disgust. On 9 October he issued an angry proclamation to the Canadians – *The Times* rechristened him 'Lord High Seditioner' – and the Government retaliated by recalling him.[57] But before the recall could arrive, Durham had left Canada.

---

[52] Throughout the Canadian mission the press either did not know of Durham's poor health or refused to let their readers know that he was under strain. Not until after his death did *The Times* grudgingly admit that this might explain some of his conduct (*The Times*, 30 July 1840). The private papers of leading politicians betray the same lack of awareness.

[53] Durham was annoyed to find this legacy awaiting him. *'They ought never to have been left for me.'* Russell later admitted he thought 'we were wrong in not disposing of the prisoners before Durham went out – but it was thought in the Cabinet impossible to try them by any other than a jury' (National Library of Scotland, Ellice Papers, E30, Durham to Ellice, Quebec, 23 June 1838, fos. 53-4; *ibid.* E49, Russell to Ellice, Cassiobury, 27 December 1838, fos. 22-3).

[54] Chester W. New, *op. cit.* pp. 387-94.

[55] *Hansard's Parliamentary Debates*, 3rd series, XLIV, 30 July 1838, cols. 755-60, and Brougham's Indemnity Bill, *ibid.* 9 August 1838, cols. 1056-1102 for second reading.

[56] *Ibid.* 3rd series, XLIV, 10 August 1838, cols. 1127-31.

[57] For the Proclamation, see Reid, *op. cit.* II, pp. 275-85; Chester W. New, *op. cit.* pp. 453-7.

Durham's defenders have insisted that he was shabbily treated by the Government and that the conduct of the Opposition was factious in the extreme. It should however be remembered that legal opinion, the opinion of the Crown's own law officers, was that the part of the Ordinance relating to Bermuda was invalid, and that this cast doubt on its general validity.[58] In those circumstances, the Government had three possible options. One was inaction. This would have been the worst possible course to follow. Doubts about the legality of the Ordinance would have grown, writs of Habeas Corpus would have been issued on behalf of the men, vexatious actions for wrongful arrest would have been brought against Government servants, and prolonged court proceedings would have undermined the mission altogether. The Government in practice had only two alternatives. The Ministers could take steps to validate the Ordinance, or end speculation by disallowing it. Those who have criticised the Whigs for not validating the Ordinance are responding as autocratically as Durham himself. The Ordinance could not have been validated simply by fiat of the Government. It would have required an Act of Parliament, and quite apart from an understandable distaste for *ex post facto* legislation, there was every sign that Parliament would give Durham no more rope. The Whigs might have attempted to by-pass Parliament by issuing an Order in Council, but this would certainly in 1838 have provoked a major constitutional clash, and Tories, Radicals and purist Whigs would certainly, and with propriety, have combined to turn out the Government on a censure motion. Two other considerations limited Melbourne's freedom. One was that Parliament had to be persuaded to pass a Bill of Indemnity. The Ordinance was legally invalid, yet servants of the Government had acted on it. The crew of the *Vixen*, which had taken the eight men to Bermuda, were liable to suits for wrongful detention. At Bermuda there would be other State employees who had acted in the natural belief that they were within the law. The Government's prior duty in these circumstances was to its junior and not its senior servants. It had to have an Indemnity Bill, and it had to accept it on Parliament's terms. And the other consideration was that the Parliamentary Session was nearing its end. It was impossible to keep members in London after the middle of August, and the Government thus had no real room for manoeuvre. At that stage in the Session, determined opposition could have blocked any measure. An attempt to tack on a validation of the Ordinance to the Indemnity would have led to the defeat of both measures. Indeed Melbourne gave way only when the

---

[58] The report of the Law Officers is quoted in Chester W. New, *op. cit.* p. 429. They seem to have gone somewhat beyond G. M. Craig's view that there were 'one or two legal flaws' in the Ordinance (G. M. Craig, editor, *op. cit.* p. iii).

Lords passed Brougham's Indemnity Bill, which specifically disallowed the Bermuda Ordinance. Not surprisingly the Ministers did not feel that they had let Durham down. 'I do not think he can fairly say you gave him up about his Ordinance, as you opposed the second reading of the Indemnity Bill', wrote Russell to Melbourne, referring to the measure which Brougham had forced on them.[59] Rather the Ministers felt that it was they who had been let down. Durham had exceeded his authority, and had failed even to supply the Government with the documents relating to the Ordinance which might have enabled them to rebut the more extreme charges of arbitrary power.[60] Durham and the Government, wrote Russell, might have broken the Lords, but the Government could not be expected to succeed on its own.[61] Of course, Melbourne might have decided to fight and go down in noble defeat, but it is difficult to see how this would have strengthened Durham's authority, how a Tory government would have furthered Durham's policies, or indeed why the Whigs should have sacrificed themselves over an issue on which they would undoubtedly have been wrong.[62]

How had it become so difficult to sustain Durham's infringement of his authority? The answer is simple. The biggest enemy of the Durham mission was not Brougham, not Melbourne, but Durham himself. Time after time the usefulness of the mission was damaged by avoidable errors of judgement on the part of the High Commissioner himself. The first mistake was Durham's decision to delay his departure for Canada until the spring. Although Buller wrote his sketch of the mission not long after Durham's death, when the tragedy of his final illness softened the criticisms of friends, he still felt that the delay in departure was 'an error most injurious to the success of the mission'. Durham accepted the appointment on 15 January, but he did not set off until 24 April. Not surprisingly, men began to take the urgency of the High Commissioner's task at his own apparent valuation. The mid-winter crossing of the Atlantic was not a pleasant one, but if Durham had hastened to Canada at once, he might have found himself better supported at home

---

59 Public Record Office, Russell Papers, PRO 30/22/3B, Russell to Melbourne (copy), Ryde, 7 September 1838, fos. 682-3.
60 Chester W. New, *op. cit.* p. 430.
61 Public Record Office, Russell Papers, PRO 30/22/3B, Russell to Melbourne (copy), Brighton, 22 October 1838, fos. 720-3.
62 The whole affair was remarkably aptly, if unconsciously, summed up by Durham himself in his argument against the continuation of absolute government in Lower Canada. 'The people of England are not accustomed to rely on the honest and discreet exercise of absolute power; and if they permit a despotism to be established in their Colonies, they feel bound, when their attention happens to be directed towards them, to watch its acts with vigilance.' C. P. Lucas, editor, *Lord Durham's Report*, II, p. 298.

when difficulties arose. 'The delay took off the bloom of the mission' was Buller's verdict.[63] Furthermore, as rumours of lavish preparations began to circulate, it seemed as if Durham was placing his personal convenience before the urgent needs of the Empire. Vanity, it seemed, was to be Durham's undoing.

Many years later Roebuck perceptively observed that he had never known anyone who 'lived so completely as he, *according to the newspapers* — His whole life was regulated by leading articles. . .'. Durham had antagonised Roebuck, himself not a modest man, by attempting to slot him into a subordinate role in the mission, with what Roebuck felt was an undue emphasis on the greater glory of the Earl of Durham.[64] But the comment is none the less true. Durham went to great lengths to strike poses and capture headlines, to engineer favourable comment. This worked where, as with the *Spectator* in 1839, Durham had the slavish Wakefield to write up his genius. But too often these public relations gestures rebounded.

As soon as Durham's appointment was announced, a rumour went round that he accepted the post only at the personal request of the Queen. 'Fudge!' was the sole comment of *The Times.*[65] The Queen, as everyone knew, was a little girl who did what Lord Melbourne told her to do. It is not difficult to guess the source of the story. Durham was remarkably sensitive about the Queen. Before her accession he had made various attempts to win her confidence — attempts to win favour with the monarch-to-be were part of the stock in trade of disgruntled politicians under the House of Hanover — and now he apparently felt some proprietary claim on the young Victoria. Certainly Melbourne and Russell were emphatic in the autumn that the Queen should not be asked to make a personal appeal to Durham to prevent his resignation. When he returned from Canada, Durham's main complaint about his treatment was the way in which the Government had used the Queen's name in disavowing him, causing Howick to comment that he seemed to think that he and the Queen were co-equal powers in the State.[66]

Another gesture which did the mission no good was Durham's grand

[63] 'Sketch of Lord Durham's Mission to Canada in 1838' in C. P. Lucas, editor, *Lord Durham's Report*, III, p. 338.
[64] University Library, Cambridge, Graham Papers (microfilm no. 42), Bundle 108, Roebuck to Graham, New Milton, Lymington, Hants, 2 June 1851; John Arthur Roebuck, *The Colonies of England: a plan for the government of some portion of our colonial possessions*, London 1849, pp. 190-2, 205n., 209n., 213n.
[65] *The Times*, 20 January 1838. See also *Sun*, 19 January 1838.
[66] Chester W. New, *op. cit.* pp. 240, 299; Public Record Office, Russell Papers, PRO 30/22/3B, Russell to Melbourne, 23 October 1838, fos. 724-5; University of Durham, Grey Papers, Journal of 3rd Earl Grey, C3/4, 15 January 1839.

announcement that he would accept no salary, merely expenses. The Tories promptly attacked this as an open-ended expense account fraud, and Stanley at least still believed this after Durham's death.[67] On his return from Canada Durham made it known that he was £10,000 out of pocket, but the nation failed to show the expected gratitude, and there were hostile questions in Parliament about the audit of his expenses.[68] This again was Durham's fault: he had lent colour to the original accusations by his free-handed spending. Even before he left for Canada, there was a hostile motion in the Commons aimed at Durham's expenditure, in which the Government came very close to defeat.[69] Vast amounts of equipment were carried across the Atlantic – plate, racing trophies, even racehorses. Durham might have been restrained from the heights of absurdity had he possessed a sense of humour: no man with a sense of humour could have made such a ceremonial entry into Quebec, in full uniform astride a white horse. Durham had a weakness for uniforms, and he created much public amusement at his own expense by taking with him three full dress uniforms of a Field Marshal. When the Bermuda Ordinance was overruled, Sir James Graham insisted that Durham would be too anxious to get more wear out of his uniforms before resigning. When Durham did resign and returned to England, he was reported by one newspaper to be walking about his house in 'his Canadian state liveries' to remind himself of his former greatness. The paragraph was headed 'Vanity'.[70] Lady Durham was reported to be lecturing the gentlemen of Canada on the styles of evening dress she was prepared to tolerate in her province. (Her private comments on colonial table-manners make this a plausible story.)[71] In fact, Durham went out of his way to court ridicule. His entourage even

---

67 'It is already plain enough, that on pretence of "accepting" no salary, Lord Durham, if he does not mean to be ruined, but merely to re-imburse his own voluntary and self-imposed charges, will be compelled to clutch twice the amount of "money" that other Governors-General have lived upon, and thought themselves amply remunerated' (*The Times*, 7 April 1838); British Museum, Peel Papers, Add. MS. 40467, Stanley to Peel, confidential, St James's Sq^r, Tuesday night (September 1842), fos. 56-7.

68 *Hansard's Parliamentary Debates*, 3rd series, XLV, 11 February, col. 214; and *ibid*. 3rd series, XLV, 21 February 1838, cols. 749-54.

69 *Hansard's Parliamentary Debates*, 3rd series, XLII, 2 April 1838, cols. 385-422. A motion by the Marquess of Chandos was defeated by only two votes.

70 University Library, Cambridge, Graham Papers (microfilm no. 30), Bundle 36, Graham to Stanley, Drayton Manor, 9 September 1838; *Morning Herald*, 12 February 1839.

71 University Library, Cambridge, Graham Papers (microfilm no. 30), Bundle 36, Graham to Stanley, Drayton Manor, 9 September 1838; Chester W. New, *op. cit.* p. 394.

included an entire orchestra, the purpose of which was unexplained until Sydney Smith pointed out that he had been sent to make overtures to the Canadians.[72] The reason why Parliament would not back the Bermuda Ordinance must be sought in the behaviour of Durham himself. He seemed to have lost all sense of proportion.

Certainly his judgement deserted him in the appointments he made. No doubt he was correct to eschew the services of the old government faction of Lower Canada, but this did not make the team of obscure, anti-Gallican carpet-baggers with whom he surrounded himself any better. Roebuck attacked them vigorously; there was Turton, a lawyer who had represented the British residents in India in their fight to be exempted from the jurisdiction of native magistrates, which could scarcely recommend him to the French; Wakefield, whose theory that colonial lands should be sold at high prices to finance colonisation was monumentally unpopular in every colony; Ellice, son of the greatest absentee landlord in Canada, who was known to the French as 'one of their bitterest, most indefatigable, and most powerful enemies'. The only colonial in the team was Adam Thom, a fierce opponent of everything French. They scarcely constituted the ideal government of Lower Canada. And Roebuck pointedly refrained from criticising their appointments on any other than public grounds.[73] Turton was an adulterer, Wakefield a child abductor. The appointment of Turton in particular saw Durham at his best and his worst. Despite Parliamentary criticism, Durham insisted on employing a friend for whose abilities he had a high regard. It is to his credit that he did not rule out a man simply because his private life had been unsuccessful. Indeed, the hypocrisy which marked the attacks on Turton is revealed by the way in which they abruptly ceased when Durham threatened to move for an inquiry into the incidence of adultery in all spheres of public life.[74] But still the appointments were ill-advised, and the splendour of the vice-regal court, to which Durham evidently attached so much value, was strangely at odds with the shabbiness of some of its members. A satirist set the whole mission in a kind of prototype Alice-in-Wonderland

---

[72] Stuart J. Reid, *op. cit.* II, pp. 164-5.

[73] Roebuck contributed a series of letters to the *Spectator*, no. 540, 3 November 1838, pp. 1039-40 (dated 1 November 1838); no. 541, 10 November 1838, pp. 1061-2 (dated 8 November); no. 542, 17 November 1838, pp. 1084-5 (dated 15 November 1838). The attack on Durham's staff was in the third letter. *The Times* had also criticised Durham for excluding Canadians from his administration (*The Times*, 9 August 1838).

[74] *Hansard's Parliamentary Debates*, 3rd series, XLV, 19 February 1838, cols. 597-600. But Lady Howick called the threat 'most offensive & blackguard'. University of Durham, Grey Papers, Journal of 3rd Earl Grey, C3/4, 19 February 1839.

world, in which two evil advisers called Gibbon and Turtle (Gibbon Wakefield and Turton) led Durham into issuing a series of outrageous ordinances, culminating with one abolishing marriage.[75] Melbourne, whose own private life was less than regular, wrote to Durham with a force unusual in him, marvelling that any man of common sense could show such a disregard for public opinion in his appointments. 'If their abilities and powers were superhuman they would not counterbalance the discredit of their characters.'[76] The sad fact is that their abilities were not superhuman. Turton, the source of so much scandal, was Durham's legal adviser and presumably it was he who failed to see that Durham had no power to exile men to Bermuda. 'We were told', wrote Charles Greville, 'that Turton's indifferent moral character was to be overlooked in favour of his great legal capacity, and now it appears that his law is not a jot better than his morals.'[77]

If Durham did little to enhance the dignity of his mission by going to Canada, he destroyed it altogether by his return to England. First there was the simple fact of resignation. Many have argued that Durham was left with little alternative but resignation, and sympathy will be felt at the all too frequent story in Canadian history of a Governor whose health had been broken by the task before him. But, none the less, Durham had resigned after scarcely five months in Canada, and it fitted too well with the picture of a vain man indignantly valuing his own conceit above the national interest. Durham's friends foresaw this from the time when he had first begun to talk of resignation. Buller, prompted by Wakefield, warned that 'in proportion to the high hopes which a nation has formed of you, and the high trust which it has reposed in you, will be the fearful recoil of its unexpected disappointment...'. It was not enough, he told Durham bluntly, to believe that he could resign simply because the Government failed to support him wholeheartedly over the appointment of Turton.[78] The arguments in this letter, written before the disallowance of the Ordinance was known, were no less applicable to that set-back than to the earlier one involving Turton. But the fact of Durham's resignation was nothing compared with the manner of it. On 9 October 1838 he issued a proclamation to the people of Canada, announcing his resignation and justifying his actions. This was certainly a bold move, and it was doubtless an honest one. But

---

[75] L. L. Sharpe, *The Viceroy's Dream, or the Canadian Government not 'wide awake'. A mono-dramatico-political poem*, London 1838.

[76] Melbourne to Durham, South Street, 18 July 1838 in Lloyd C. Sanders, editor, *op. cit.* pp. 428-9.

[77] (Henry Reeve, editor), *A Journal of the Reign of Queen Victoria from 1837 to 1852 (The Greville Memoirs)* (3 vols.) London 1885, I, p. 123.

[78] Buller to Durham, 7 September 1838, in Chester W. New, *op. cit.* pp. 422-7.

it was also unprecedented, and caused great scandal in England. His closest friends and relatives were strongest in their condemnation – Lord Grey thought he had lost his head completely, while Ellice wrote to say he hoped no such document would ever be issued again.[79] Howick blamed Durham's 'childish impatience' and described the Proclamation as 'most indecent'.[80] These men were not Durham's enemies. If Durham had wished to make a public defence of his conduct, the proper place for it was the House of Lords. Yet the same historians who have praised the undoubted dignity with which Durham refused to be drawn into such parliamentary fighting on his return, have been remarkably kind in their treatment of the Proclamation. No doubt it proceeded from 'his *flair* for the dramatic',[81] but all acts, and dramatic ones in particular, are likely to produce consequences. If a colonial Governor formally and publicly informs the people of his colony that he is giving up his Governorship in disgust because their true interests are being sacrificed to the play of party factions at home, it is at least plausible that they might interpret it as advice that they too should throw off their colonial status in disgust. Certainly Durham had violated that basic convention which requires a man leaving office to do nothing which could embarrass his successor. Howick took particular exception to Durham's last minute appointment of James Stuart as Chief Justice of Lower Canada, which he feared was 'dictated by a wish to embarrass us knowing as he must the extreme difficulty of either confirming or cancelling such an appointment'. But it was the Proclamation which attracted general disapproval. Both Howick and Russell felt that by issuing it he had destroyed a reasonably strong case in his own defence.[82]

Nor did it escape the notice of his critics that Durham had stalked out of Canada in advance of his official recall, only two days before a second revolt broke out. The authorities had been aware for several months that another outbreak was brewing, and the defence offered by Durham's apologists, that he had not wanted to be in the way of Sir John Colborne, the Commander-in-Chief, was not the strongest imaginable.[83] In fact Colborne was anxious to get Durham out of the way, in

[79] Chester W. New, *op. cit.* p. 456; National Library of Scotland, Ellice Papers, E30, Ellice to Durham (copy), December 1838, fos. 74-6.

[80] University of Durham, Grey Papers, Journal of 3rd Earl Grey, C3/3, 7 November 1838.

[81] Chester W. New, *op. cit.* p. 453.

[82] National Library of Scotland, Ellice Papers, E22, Howick to Ellice, private, War Office, 23 November 1838, fos. 37-8; *ibid.* E49, Russell to Ellice, Cassiobury, 20 December 1838, fos. 20-1.

[83] Chester W. New, *op. cit.* p. 469, and see *The Times*, 22 October 1838; *Examiner*, no. 1611, 16 December 1838, p. 785.

C

order to avoid any friction between his own military authority and the civil power which he was due to take over. None the less, the coincidence was 'awkward' for a Government which had suffered enough from its High Commissioner.[84] Remarkably the Opposition's capacity for shock was still not exhausted. Peel felt it was 'scandalous' that Durham should have run away knowing that another revolt was brewing, but his disgust was mingled with 'a feeling of Gratitude to him for coming away, and leaving the administration of the Province in much better hands'.[85] The only person who seemed unembarrassed by the coincidence was the ex-Governor himself. He landed at Plymouth on 30 November, and began a progress across Devon, announcing the success of his mission in reply to the addresses made to him by the radicals of the country towns he passed through. At Exeter news of the revolt caught up with him, casting some doubt on his reiterated claims. Russell felt that Durham should either have resigned quietly or have remained at his post, where he would have gained the credit for suppressing the second revolt. 'But his leaving his post at Quebec to boast of his success at Plymouth, just when the rebellion broke out afresh, has lowered him in the eyes of all men of sense.'[86] Lady Howick came to the more forthright conclusion that 'his vanity has driven away his wits'.[87]

At every stage there had been errors of judgement, on a scale which utterly discredited the mission in the eyes of contemporaries. If anything Durham's stock was at its lowest in the eyes of the Ministers who had appointed him, the men to whom his Report would be most immediately directed. Their private correspondence betrays the maximum of irritation at Durham, but at no point is there any evidence of awareness of the main point in his defence – the break-down of health. Consequently nothing relieved the harshness of their comments. 'What he did was often right, but always so done as to be totally indefensible', was the conclusion of Melbourne, who came to think that Durham's

---

84 Chester W. New, *op. cit.* p. 470; Melbourne to Russell, n.p., 4 December 1838 in Lloyd C. Sanders, editor, *op. cit.* p. 440.

85 University Library, Cambridge, Graham Papers (microfilm no. 30), Bundle 36, Peel to Graham, Drayton Manor, 5 December (1838). 'First it shews that he ran away from Canada with a full knowledge that Confusion was impending, and secondly that the Conspiracy was hatched without the possibility of reference to the Proceedings of Lord Brougham and the House of Lords.'

86 National Library of Scotland, Ellice Papers, E49, Russell to Ellice, Cassiobury, 20 December 1838, fos. 20-1.

87 University of Durham, Grey Papers, Journal of 3rd Earl Grey, C3/3, 7 December 1838 (entry by Lady Howick). The progress through Devon is described in Chester W. New, *op. cit.* pp. 479-81.

appointment was the greatest blunder he had ever made.[88] By August 1838 Melbourne was predicting that Durham would concoct a general arrangement within two months, return home boasting of its success and, if it collapsed, claim that it was all because of the way he had been treated.[89] By October Melbourne had the gloomy pleasure of seeing his predictions beginning to come true. 'He made large promises, all of which, he will now say, he should have fulfilled if he had been permitted to remain.'[90] Durham had indeed made some extravagant claims. Provided the Government backed him, he assured Glenelg, 'I will answer for handing over to you in a few months all the North American provinces in a state of loyalty and contentment'. He had been in the Canadas less than a month before announcing to Melbourne that they were 'saved to England, as far as I am concerned. . .'.[91] Statements on this extravagant scale could inspire little confidence but much foreboding. Russell had sardonically anticipated the possibility that Durham might resign and return home — 'perhaps he may think there is an opening for a moderate Radical'. But nearly a week after learning that Durham had resigned, Russell evidently did not believe that he would really go through with a step which 'was hasty & ill-considered'.[92] Consequently when he did carry out his intention, he received a chilly reception from the Government. Durham began a lofty feud with the Ministers, and Lady Durham energetically joined in, resigning her post in the Bedchamber and rebutting the overtures of her sister-in-law, Lady Howick, with an icy coolness.[93] In Whig society this was war to the knife.

Early in December Melbourne suggested to Russell that they should communicate with their ex-Commissioner, to ask if he had any urgent information to give. Russell agreed, adding tartly that if Durham replied in the negative 'he would seem to confess that his departure from

---

[88] David Cecil, *Lord M, or the later Life of Lord Melbourne* (London 1962 ed.), pp. 191-2.

[89] Melbourne to Russell, South Street, 25 August 1838, in Lloyd C. Sanders, editor, *op. cit.* pp. 432-3.

[90] Melbourne to Thomson, Windsor Castle, 30 October 1838, in *ibid.* pp. 436-8.

[91] Durham to Glenelg, 15 June 1838, Durham to Melbourne, 15 June 1838, in Chester W. New, *op. cit.* pp. 385-6.

[92] Public Record Office, Russell Papers, PRO 30/22/3B, Russell to Melbourne (copy), Ryde, 7 September 1838, fos. 682-3; *ibid.* Russell to Melbourne (copy), Brighton, 23 October 1838, fos. 724-5.

[93] The feud can be followed in University of Durham, Grey Papers, Journal of 3rd Earl Grey, C3/3, 8, 14 December 1838, C3/4, 24 December 1838, 14, 15, 22, 26 January 1839. Durham had no doubts about his conduct. 'They ought to have recollected in their treatment of me that I was the Equal of all, & superior of many of them' (National Library of Scotland, Ellice Papers, E30, Durham to Ellice, private, Cleveland Row, 1 January 1839, fos. 77-8).

Canada was such a blessing to the Province that he could not delay it till he received the answer of the Govt'. The Ministers were not in fact interested in any information they might receive from Durham, but wished merely to cover themselves 'as he wd otherwise make a handle of not having *been* asked & as he professes in his speeches to have such important disclosures to make. . . '.[94] 'Durham at the same time was trying to play the ball into the Government's court by offering to give them any information they might require.[95] Eventually, though, he had to fall back on the promise that his Report would provide 'all the information which you can require in order to enable you to form a correct opinion as to the state of the North American provinces'. Glenelg replied, carefully rubbing in the fact that Durham had 'not suggested any particular points with respect to Canada on which you consider it of importance that you should communicate immediate information' and declining to raise any questions himself since 'you lead me to expect that your report will shortly be completed. . .'.[96] In fact there is no sign at all that the Ministers were anxiously waiting for their ex-Governor to pronounce.[97] A week before Christmas Melbourne wrote, 'I do not expect much from Durham's suggestions. I understand now that he himself says he has no plan to propose, and if he gives us general observations he will not advance us much upon our journey'.[98]

There is one further point which should be made at this stage — one raised at the time but little noticed since.[99] When Durham sat down to write the Report in December 1838, he had no right to expect that it

----

[94] Melbourne to Russell, Downing Street, 8 December 1838 in Lloyd C. Sanders, editor, *op. cit.* pp. 440-1; Public Record Office, Russell Papers, PRO 30/22/3C, Russell to Melbourne (copy), Cassiobury, 9 December 1838, fos. 851-2; University of Durham, Grey Papers, Journal of 3rd Earl Grey, C3/3, 7 December 1838.

[95] Public Record Office, CO 42/284, Durham to Sir George Grey, Cleveland Row, 20 December 1838, between fos. 431-2.

[96] *Ibid.* CO 42/284, Durham to Glenelg, Cleveland Row, 20 December 1838, fo. 432; Glenelg to Durham (copy), no. 82, Downing-street, 26 December 1838, fo. 434.

[97] They merely insisted that Durham had a duty to explain himself. 'No man ever served the Queen, & withheld an explanation of his conduct from the Queen's servants.' (National Library of Scotland, Ellice Papers, E49, Russell to Ellice, Cassiobury, 24 December 1838, fos. 24-5.)

[98] Melbourne to Russell, Downing Street, 19 December 1838, in Lloyd C. Sanders, editor, *op. cit.* pp. 443-4.

[99] E.g. *Quarterly Review*, LXIII, March 1839, pp. 506-8; Public Archives of Canada, Derby Paper, microfilm A30, 8, memorandum by Sir Francis Head, 62 Park St, Grosvenor Square, 25 May 1839. Head claimed that the doctrines of the Report 'were not produced or even concocted untill Lord Durham was "functus officii" and untill having abandoned his post, he had merged into, and become one of the public'.

would be treated as a public document. In so far as he had ever possessed the power to deliver such a document — and even if this was disputed — he had surrendered it on resigning his post, thereby rendering null the commission and instructions with which he had held it. Durham could not attempt to resign that part of his post relating to the Government of Canada and at the same time insist on maintaining the right to prepare an official report — though it was very like him to try. Any report written by Durham in December 1838 and January 1839 was the work of a private citizen, and the Government would be under no obligation to treat it as an official document, and under even less compulsion to make it public.

3   THE RECEPTION OF THE REPORT

In the event, the Government was never given the option to withhold the Report from the public. On Friday 8 February the main conclusions appeared in twelve and a half very long columns of *The Times*. A further twenty columns appeared the next day, and nineteen and a quarter on the Monday.[1] Fifty-two long columns of very small print was a lot to take in at three breakfast times, and the reader's task of assimilating the Report was not made easier by *The Times'* anxiety to clinch its scoop by printing the conclusion first. Other papers followed suit, publishing even more indigestible extracts to catch up.[2] Small wonder that Charles Greville, the diarist, commented only on the length of the document.[3] There can be little doubt that the Durham Report failed to make the impact which its author had wished for. This is not to deny that it created a sensation. The *Colonial Gazette* felt that the Report 'deserves and has met with a degree of attention, on the part of the public, greater, perhaps, than has been given to any other state-paper of modern times'.[4] Whilst this article has a certain family resemblance to productions of the Durham public relations machine, its evidence can be supported by the fact that an unofficial edition of the Report was published immediately afterwards, including a selection

---

[1] *The Times*, 8, 9, 11 February 1839.
[2] E.g. *Morning Chronicle*, 9, 11 February 1839; *Standard*, 8, 9, 11 February 1839.
[3] H. Reeve, editor, *The Greville Memoirs*, I, pp. 162-3. Durham himself adopted a cavalier attitude to those who might object to the length of the Report, writing that 'it is of such vital importance that the subject should be *for the first time* fairly stated, & British Interests prominently brought forward that they must not grumble at the time taken or the amount of what they will have to read & digest' (National Library of Scotland, Ellice Papers, E30, Durham to Ellice, private, Cleveland Row, 18 January 1839, fos. 79-80).
[4] *Colonial Gazette* no. 16, 16 February 1839, pp. 185-6.

from his official correspondence.⁵ But the public interest which surrounded the Report did not amount to an intelligent interest in the
Report itself. The public seems to have been more interested in
Durham's relations with the Ministers, and whether the Report would
be the occasion for a reconciliation or a further quarrel. The circumstances surrounding the Report were a good deal more exciting than its
lengthy analysis of the problems of a distant colony. What is of most
importance is that neither in the newspapers nor in the magazines and
reviews did the Durham Report receive anything like an extended
public discussion. Lord Bryce was later to argue that public opinion was
not formed simply by men's reactions to events, but was a more com-
plicated process of discussing and digesting the more sophisticated
viewpoints put forward in their newspapers. Both de Tocqueville and
Cornewall Lewis agreed on the power of the Press to shape opinions in
early nineteenth-century England, and it is evident that the basis of an
informed public opinion must be an intelligent discussion of issues both
in the Press and Parliament.⁶ The Durham Report was never specifically
discussed in Parliament and certainly received nothing like an extended
or intelligent discussion in the Press. Its reception in the newspapers
followed a simple pattern: the Report was vigorously abused by the
Tory press, without any particular reference to the text, while it received at best lukewarm commendation from the liberal and radical
side. The only exception to the pattern, the extravagant praise of the
Spectator, can be shown to be an exercise in special pleading. There
may have been great public interest in the Report as a political event,
but so far as its specific recommendations went, it was a failure. Attention has already been drawn by Grace Fox to its poor reception in a
selection of British newspapers and reviews. Indeed, Miss Fox, who
believed in the Report's central importance in British imperial history,
was strong in her condemnation of the hostility and indifference with
which it was received.⁷ Here it is suggested that the immediate reception of the Report was more unfavourable even than was suggested
by Miss Fox, and that the extent to which it was rejected by contem-

---

⁵ *The Report and Despatches of The Earl of Durham, Her Majesty's High
Commissioner and Governor-General of British North America*, London 1839.
This is 'Ridgway's edition' referred to by Charles Buller in his account of the
mission (C. P. Lucas, editor, *Lord Durham's Report*, III, p. 361).
⁶ James Bryce, *The American Commonwealth* (3 vols.), London 1888, III, pp.
24-32; Alexis de Tocqueville, *Democracy in America* (4 vols.), (translated by
Henry Reeve), London 1835-40, Part the Second, III, pp. 229-36; George
Cornewall Lewis, *An Essay on the Influence of Authority in matters of
opinion*, London 1849, pp. 342-50.
⁷ Grace Fox, 'The Reception of Lord Durham's Report in the English Press',
Canadian Historical Review, XVI, 1935, pp. 276-88.

poraries goes far towards destroying the case for its long-term importance.

The traditional view of the Report has assumed that it had an immediate educative effect on the public, which was seen first in the early acceptance of the Union of the Canadas but which was to lie at the bottom of all subsequent developments. If it can be shown that the Report had a very poor reception, and did not become a basis for a sympathetic and informed discussion of colonial government, then it becomes correspondingly harder to discover the subsequent point at which it was rediscovered and became a formative influence on British policy. In fact its rediscovery did not come until after the problems it had discussed had passed into history, and it became a decorative rather than a formative document in imperial history.

One reason why the Report failed to produce the editorial discussion necessary for the creation of informed opinion can be sought in the newspapers themselves. By modern standards they were poorly designed, crowding their columns with verbatim transcripts of speeches and documents in a small print which made heavy demands on the reader. Thus the publication of the Report in this way was nothing exceptional. An attempt to present this mass of material in a form palatable to the reader was made in the leading articles, which generally filled several columns and which were better written and frequently set in clearer type. Only in the leading article could the reader learn in an abridged form what was going on, and what he should think about it. But by convention the leading article followed the event at a day's interval, allowing time for editorial reflection. Now the publication of the Durham Report in *The Times* had already spanned four days – Friday to Monday – in jumbled order, and a news story cannot be kept alive for ever. Newspapers were reluctant to comment at all until they had the entire document, and reluctant to comment in detail without closer study. *The Times* itself remarked that it was more a dissertation than a report, and asserted that it would be 'absurd and presumptuous' to give its verdict straight away.[8] Other newspapers postponed comment for the same reason, and in many cases this was to be postponement *sine die.*[9] Other stories were to fill the newspapers, and the pressure of current affairs never gave editors the chance to deliver leisurely analysis of a document that was rapidly receding into the past. Under these circumstances, brief but savage attacks would have the advantage over detailed defence.

[8] *The Times*, 13 February 1839.
[9] *Colonial Gazette*, no. 11, 9 February 1839, p. 168; *Examiner*, no. 1619, 10 February 1839, pp. 90-1; *Globe*, 8 February 1839; *Manchester Guardian*, 9 February 1839.

A second reason for the lame reception of the Report was that its author had attempted to over-sell it in advance. In his early speeches to the radicals of Devon, Durham had given the impression that he would have world-shaking revelations to make. His coterie had been active in boosting the Report in advance of its publication — before it was even written. In the *Westminster Review* John Stuart Mill ended a long defence of Durham's rule of Canada with some advance praise of the Report.[10] (The *Westminster* carried no such praise after the actual appearance of the Report.) 'We all thought we recognised an article in the Examiner as having proceeded from Cleveland Row,' wrote Lady Howick in mid-December 1838. 'It was very moderate in its tone & professions but immoderately extolling Lord Durham as one about to offer a new & bright example to be inscribed in the page of history — one who sacrificed his private resentment for the good of the country!' To which Lady Howick added that much used expletive 'Fudge!'.[11] There can be little doubt that this extravagant advance build-up of the Report played into the hands of opponents and embarrassed those who might have supported Durham. Where were these '*astonishing revelations*', trumpeted the Tories, where were the '*inconceivable disclosures*' which had been promised?[12] It did not need a particularly close reading of the conclusions published in the first extract in *The Times* to see that Durham had failed to break any new ground. The salient points which immediately stood out — Canadian union and local self-government — were not very novel. The leader writer of one Tory paper confessed that he had read the extracts in *The Times* 'with considerable distrust' but had found little that was new in them.[13] Another called the Report 'a prolix document' which 'tells nothing that has not been told, and generally much better told before, except for a few crotchets of Lord Durham's own, which will pass for what they are worth'.[14] 'The most important practical suggestion contained in it has not even the merit of originality,' claimed another — which like some other critics thought Durham was proposing an immediate legislative union of all the colonies. The writer had been too angry to read closely a document 'so portentously prosy, pedantic and prolix, so offensively

10 *London and Westminster Review*, XXXII, 1838, pp. 241-60. For the connection between Mill and the Durham group, see National Library of Scotland, Ellice Papers, E5, Buller to Ellice, Quebec, 29 September 1838, fos. 16-21.

11 University of Durham, Grey Papers, Journal of 3rd Earl Grey, C3/3, 16 December 1838, entry by Lady Howick. The article is in *Examiner*, no. 1611, 16 December 1838, p. 785.

12 *Quarterly Review*, LXIII, March 1839, p. 523.

13 *Morning Herald*, 9 February 1839.

14 *Standard*, 12 February 1839.

arrogant, egotistical, and inconclusive'.[15] *The Times* eventually complimented the industry behind the Report but concluded that 'as a whole it furnishes evidence of the most incorrigible prejudice respecting principles and questions of the highest moment...'.[16] If the Duke of Wellington had written the Durham Report, then the Tories might have been convinced by its arguments. But Durham was known to everyone as a radical, and as soon as it appeared that the much vaunted Report was no more than a vivid recital of known radical complaints, the Tories fell upon it. The *Morning Post* spoke for them all when it dismissed the Durham Report with the comment that it was 'as worthless as it is wordy – in short just such a State paper as might have been expected from such a statesman as the Earl of Durham'.[17]

Such comments as were made on the Report after its immediate publication again came from the Tories. Between 18 and 26 February *The Times* published a series of open letters to Durham from 'A Colonist' – T. C. Haliburton, an arch-Tory from Nova Scotia. Unfortunately Haliburton was another critic whose anger prevented him from establishing what exactly Durham was proposing, and his contribution was very far from constituting a basis for informed public discussion.[18] Nor did the magazines and reviews make good the deficiency. A short and near hysterical assault on 'that rank and infectious Report' in the most influential of them, the *Quarterly*, made little attempt at a detailed analysis, while the two other magazines to discuss the subject were also critical but much less influential.[19]

These attacks on the Report would have been less damaging had the liberal side in politics not allowed them to be virtually conclusive. The most striking aspect of the reception of the Report was not the predictable crescendo of outrage from the Tories, which can be documented and established by quotation – but the almost total silence of those who might have been expected to support Durham's ideas – and silence does not lend itself to quotation. A partial exception was the *Leeds Mercury* which hailed the Report as 'the boldest, most masterly, most

[15] *Metropolitan Conservative Journal*, 16 February 1839.
[16] *The Times*, 18 February 1839.
[17] *Morning Post*, 18 February 1839. The *Post* had earlier called for the appointment of the Duke of Wellington as Governor General (26 December 1837).
[18] *The Times*, 18, 19, 20, 21, 22, 25, 26 February, reprinted as *A Reply to the Report of the Earl of Durham. By a Colonist*, London 1839.
[19] *Quarterly Review*, LXIII, March 1839, pp. 505-25; *Dublin University Magazine*, XIII, March 1839, pp. 355-68; *Canadian, British American, and West Indian Magazine*, I, March 1839, pp. 56-73. It is strange that an event long regarded as so important should have been neglected by the *Edinburgh Review*, the *Westminster Review*, the *Eclectic Review*, *Fraser's Magazine*, the *British and Foreign Review* and apparently every other periodical of influence.

interesting State Paper we remember to have read for some time'. It predicted that 'the official and especially the Tory party' would be scared by 'its grandeur and consistency' but even so found room for only 'a very brief and hasty sketch of Lord Durham's magnificent plan'. In subsequent issues the paper did not return to the subject.[20] The *Morning Chronicle*, which was close to the Government, did go as far as to say that circulation of the Report would do good, but added that in so wide a field Durham could hardly be expected to convert everyone.[21] It was scarcely a red-blooded defence, but it was about as good as the Report was to get. It is strange that in the *Examiner*, the *Westminster Review*, the *Edinburgh Review*, the *Globe* and the *Manchester Guardian* — a powerful section of the country's leading liberal and radical journals — the Report received at most a brief murmur of praise. Even in the *Westminster* and the *Examiner*, which had hailed the Report in advance, there was no discussion of its recommendations — barely even a mention.

The omission is all the more striking when it is compared with the books which did get reviewed in the pages of the journals. The *Eclectic* and the *Monthly Review* gave space to Sir Francis Head's *Narrative*[22] rather than to the Durham Report, against which Head's book was aimed. The *Eclectic Review*, in criticising Head, did also complain that 'his narrative has been highly lauded by some ministerial papers, as affording a useful counterpoise to what they are pleased to consider the injudicious radicalism of Lord Durham's report'.[23] This rebuttal of Head's account of the past was no substitute for an essay on Durham's view of the future. The *Dublin Review* and the *Edinburgh Review* found space for Marryat's *Diary*,[24] as did the *Quarterly*, the only one of the three to give coverage to the Durham Report. The *Dublin* and the *Quarterly* coupled Marryat with the Hon. C. A. Murray's *Travels in North America*.[25] These were both minor works. Murray's book was little more than the traveller's tales suggested in its title. Marryat attempted to be more serious, prompting the *Edinburgh* to comment

20 *Leeds Mercury*, 16 February 1839. But the *Leeds Mercury* had more than half promised to support any plan which Durham might put forward, on 8 December 1838.
21 *Morning Chronicle*, 9 February 1839.
22 Francis B. Head, *A Narrative*, London 1839. Quotations are made from the third edition.
23 *Eclectic Review*, n.s. V, January-June 1839, pp. 556-71, esp. p. 558; *Monthly Review*, n.s. I, April 1839, pp. 596-7.
24 Captain Marryat, *A Diary in America with remarks on its institutions* (3 vols.), London 1839.
25 C. A. Murray, *Travels in North America during the years 1834, 1835 and 1836* (2 vols.), London 1839.

that the only literary effort it could imagine to equal the disaster of
Marryat on American politics would be a sea novel by de Tocqueville.[26]
The failure of the periodicals to deal extensively with the Durham
Report can hardly be put down to a reluctance to give space to North
American subjects. The liberals simply made no effort to defend the
Report, so the public debate took the form of a walk-over for the
Tories.

One contributory reason for this silence was a split which had developed between Durham and most of the Radicals. Only the light-
weight Molesworth actively took his part, while Roebuck, the most
knowledgeable of them in Canadian matters, was engaged in a personal
and political quarrel. The radicals apparently felt that Durham had
deserted them by accepting the mission at all, and so, said Roebuck to
Hobhouse in January 1838, 'we must trot out the old horse'.[27] Since
the 'old horse' was Brougham, it is not surprising that they found
themselves in opposition to Durham. But this is only part of the explanation. The real reason for the silence of the liberal and radical press
was that Durham had totally discredited himself. The radicals had other
battles to fight — they were supporters of reform, supporters of
economy, opponents of aristocratic control. Certainly they were concerned about the colonies, but they were only one battle-field in an
overall campaign, and no one will wish to get drawn into battle against
the odds. The Report was the outcome of a mission which had gone
disastrously and unnecessarily astray at every point. Neither the liberals
nor the radicals were keen to jeopardise their overall political fortunes
by fighting a hopeless battle on behalf of a man to whom neither group
felt particularly grateful. Moreover, neither the traditional Whigs nor
the Parliamentary group of Radicals could back the Report wholeheartedly — the former were suspicious of colonial self-government, but
the latter by and large hostile to the Union of the Canadas. Here, it may
be argued, Durham suffered because he was impartial, precisely because
he did refuse to be the voice of one party. No doubt this argument can
be used, but the reluctance of the anti-Tory groups to make much even
of the parts of the Report with which they could agree, suggests much

---

[26] *Dublin Review*, VII, November 1839, pp. 399-429; *Edinburgh Review*, LXX,
October 1839, pp. 123-49; *Quarterly Review*, LXIX, October 1839, pp.
308-31.

[27] For Molesworth, see University of Durham, Grey Papers, Journal of 3rd Earl
Grey, C3/3, 7 December 1838 and Molesworth's speech at Leeds, 5 February
1840 in H. E. Egerton, editor, *Selected Speeches of Sir William Molesworth,
Bart., P.C., M.P., on questions relating to colonial policy*, London 1903, pp.
84-5. For Roebuck, see J. A. Roebuck, *The Colonies of England*, pp. 191-2,
and Broughton, *Recollections*, V, p. 116 (18 January 1838).

more that Durham's own behaviour was regarded as indefensible by those closest to him in politics.

There was one exception to the general reluctance to defend the Report, but it was an exception which did little good to its own cause. The Report, and more especially its author, were lauded in the *Spectator* but even so there seems to have been little attempt at a reasoned discussion of its recommendations. Durham himself was hailed as 'the manly advocate of natural justice; the proud rejecter of selfish, although common and recognised, expedients of conduct; the sincere despiser, and fearless opponent, of the cant and hypocrisy of public life'.[28] One can almost hear the chorus of 'Fudge!' This is a little too fulsome to be regarded as an objective judgement. As early as January 1837 Howick had learnt that the *Spectator* was under the control 'of that clever scoundrel Gibbon Wakefield'.[29] There can be little doubt that the *Spectator*'s slavish support for Durham in 1839 stemmed from the same source. In 1838, while Wakefield had been in Canada, away from the *Spectator* office, the magazine had published Roebuck's attack on Durham, and had itself even described 'the manly advocate of natural justice' as 'that silly unstatesmanlike Utopian personage'.[30] In 1839 it was very obvious that Wakefield was back. But like so many of Durham's earlier public relations gestures, this one failed. The *Morning Post* expressed its disgust at the way the Report was being 'so outrageously puffed by Lord Durham's retainers in the newspapers'. The *Post* complained that Durham was having his 'bundle of balderdash' written up like a miracle pimple plaster. 'Lord Durham wants that a prodigious fuss should be made about himself and his observations, and, lest his tedious Report should not be enough, he has puffers at work in all directions, to tell bragging and fantastical lies about it.'[31] The *Spectator*'s fulsome praise only drew attention to the sheer arrogance with which Durham appeared to assume that only he could solve the problems of Canada.

The failure of the Report to make any real impact must be very largely attributed to the way in which Durham had discredited himself. This tended to encourage attention to other aspects of the Durham saga, and there were elements of bad luck as well as bad judgement behind its failure. The form of publication, in reverse order spread over three issues of *The Times*, certainly did not help any attempt to sustain interest in the text itself. But the form of publication was nothing to

28 *Spectator*, no. 556, 23 February 1839, pp. 182-3.
29 University of Durham, Grey Papers, Journal of 3rd Earl Grey, C3/2, 15 January 1837.
30 *Spectator*, no. 538, 20 October 1838, p. 988.
31 *Morning Post*, 20 February 1839.

the manner of it. Even four years later, a rare mention of the Report in official correspondence could prompt the Colonial Secretary to remark that its 'unauthorised publication ... was most unfortunate' before even the briefest reference to its contents.[32] The most reliable tradition suggests that Wakefield was responsible for the leak to *The Times*, and if this is so, he, like Turton, had signally failed to offset the liability of his private character by any service to Durham.[33] For Wakefield, himself involved in journalism, ought to have realised that serious consideration of the Report would be elbowed aside by the sensational 'human interest' story provided by the circumstances of its appearance. Certainly a large amount of ink and energy was wasted on this aspect of the affair. The only sensible comment was the remark of the *Morning Post* that considering the type of people Durham had around him, nothing that happened was really surprising. Others too thought of the 'raffs' in Durham's entourage, and were not surprised.[34] The manner in which the Report appeared revived all too vividly memories of the blundering mission with which it was associated. It appeared in the worst possible circumstances for sympathetic consideration of its ideas.

The first 'human interest' story was rapidly succeeded by another. Durham had been critical of Sir Francis Head, the former Lieutenant-Governor of Upper Canada. Head, never a modest or cautious man, wrote publicly to Melbourne demanding the right to publish his despatches in order to rebut Durham's charges.[35] Without waiting for Government approval, he published his *Narrative*, based largely on unauthorised extracts from his despatches.[36] Once again a sensational story of personalities pushed aside dry analyses.

The timing of the publication of the Report was unlucky in that it coincided with the fall from office of Lord Glenelg, the Colonial Secretary. On 9 February, when the newspapers might have given some attention to the extract of the Report published in the previous day's *Times*, they were in fact devoting their columns to stories that Glenelg had been pitched out of the Cabinet after a joint threat of resignation by Russell and Howick, a story which was of overriding news value,

---

[32] Public Record Office, CO 537/141, Stanley to Metcalfe, copy, private, Downing Street, 29 May 1843, fos. 5-20, and see draft in CO 537/142, fos. 26-42. The subject was raised by Metcalfe (CO 537/142, Metcalfe to Stanley, confidential, no. 1, Kingston, 24 April 1843, fos. 6-25).

[33] See the note by Henry Reeve in Reeve, editor, *The Greville Memoirs,* II, p. 163n.

[34] *Morning Post,* 9 February 1839; University of Durham, Grey Papers, Journal of 3rd Earl Grey, C3/4, 8 February 1839 (entry by Lady Howick).

[35] F. B. Head to Melbourne, Athenaeum, 13 February 1839, in *The Times,* 14 February 1839.

[36] Francis B. Head, *A Narrative,* London 1839.

especially as it happened to be true.[37] The publication of the Report and the resignation of Glenelg were stories in direct competition with each other, and it is not surprising that the colonial story with the more immediate impact on home politics tended to take precedence.

The fact that Glenelg's resignation coincided with the appearance of what many have regarded as a blueprint for a new colonial policy, does provide a problem for those wishing to argue that the Report influenced the Government. *The Times* had guessed that Melbourne might offer the vacant place to Durham, and certainly the Ministers had considered making him Colonial Secretary in the summer of 1837.[38] If they had intended to base their Canadian policy on the Report, it is strange that they should have offered the Colonies not to Durham, who was once again in good health and capable of doing the work, but to the Marquess of Normanby – who does not seem to have wanted the job, and was soon to give it up.[39] It is true that Normanby's son, Lord Mulgrave, had accompanied Durham to Canada as aide-de-camp, but Mulgrave, a teenage army officer, seems to have played only a minor ceremonial role on the fringe of the mission.[40] This is too tenuous a connection to argue that Normanby was in any way politically committed to Durham, and in any case his short-lived appointment was no substitute for that of Durham himself.

One further explanation for the Report's lack of impact lies in the fact that it was only part of a sea of papers on Canada. Once again, fitting the Report into its historical context reduces the claims which may be made for it. By February 1839 the British public had endured a fifteen month Canadian crisis, over problems which were not new. It may be guessed that the public appetite for tomes on Canada had already declined into insignificance. In September 1837, for instance, *The Times* had published an exchange of letters between Papineau and the Governor's Civil Secretary, adding: 'We give these documents as forming part of the history of the times, not that we believe they possess any particular interest here...'[41] Six months later the *Sun* received a report of the Legislative Council of Upper Canada, but refused to print such 'silly, contradictory, impertinent rubbish' because not one

---

37 E.g. *The Times*, 9 February 1839; *Morning Post*, 9 February 1839.
38 *The Times*, 9 February 1839, and also *Colonial Gazette*, no. 7, 12 January 1839, p. 104; University of Durham, Grey Papers, Journal of 3rd Earl Grey, C3/2, 20 June 1837.
39 J. A. Hamilton, 'Constantine Henry Phipps, First Marquess of Normanby', in *Dictionary of National Biography*, XLV, pp. 230-1.
40 Major Richardson, *Eight Years in Canada*, New York 1967 (reprint of 1847 ed.), pp. 45-6.
41 *The Times*, 13 September 1837.

subscriber in a thousand would read it.[42] The public appetite was perhaps more generally limited than has been thought. When in 1844 the Colonial Office received a pamphlet of 180 pages written in defence of Metcalfe by Egerton Ryerson, Stephen commented that 'so long a Pamphlet on any subject of the day w^d be laid aside in this Country as too long to be read. . .'.[43] The British people were not indifferent to the colonial connection, but they were not enthusiastic about keeping abreast of thick volumes on colonial politics. And in the first two months of 1839 there was plenty to choose from. Ten days before the Report appeared, T. C. Haliburton published his *Bubbles of Canada.*[44] Haliburton was a colonial Tory who had recently become widely known in Britain as the creator of Sam Slick, a home-spun Yankee story-teller whose adventures were to fill a series of novels, all now deservedly forgotten. The title, *Bubbles of Canada*, seems to have been an attempt to mislead the public into thinking that this too was a humorous work. In fact it was an attempt to kill in advance anything Durham might propose by proving that all radicals and French Canadians were irredeemably wicked. It achieved an unparalleled level of tedium but, all the same, its arguments were rehearsed in three very long leading articles of *The Times* — more than the Durham Report was to receive.[45] The Report itself followed a week later, and did not, of course, shelter behind a misleading title. Then the Government published both the Report and two hundred and sixty-nine of Durham's despatches, some of which found their way into the newspapers.[46] The despatches did Durham little good: Charles Greville commented that the despatches illustrated his arrogance, and that Glenelg had the better of the exchanges.[47] On 18 February Sir Francis Head published his highly idiosyncratic *Narrative*, a work of compelling scurrility.[48] Thus in little more than three weeks, eighteen hundred pages of basic text in four publications had been presented to the public — surely a surfeit

[42] *Sun*, 22 March 1838.
[43] Public Record Office, CO 42/518, Minute by Stephen, 16 September 1844, on Metcalfe to Stanley, no. 138, Government House, Montreal, 27 August 1844, fos. 202-3. The pamphlet, Egerton Ryerson, *Sir Charles Metcalfe Defended against the attacks of his late counsellors*, Toronto 1844, is at fos. 204-97.
[44] [T. C. Haliburton], *The Bubbles of Canada. By the author of 'The Clockmaker'*, London 1839.
[45] *The Times*, 30, 31 January, 1 February 1839. For comments on the title, V. L. O. Chittick, *Thomas Chandler Haliburton ('Sam Slick') A Study in Provincial Toryism*, New York 1924, pp. 241-3.
[46] Parliamentary Papers, 1839, XXXII, 2, pp. 1-690. See also *The Times*, 14 February 1839; *Examiner*, no. 1620, 17 February 1839, pp. 99-100.
[47] Reeve, editor, *The Greville Memoirs*, II, p. 165.
[48] *The Times*, 18 February 1839.

even for the most avid colonial enthusiast. Sir Francis Head himself hoped only that the *Narrative* would 'find its own level among the mass of Reports and Documents which are already struggling to obtain the consideration of the public'.[49] For in addition to the four main publications, there were a number of lesser pamphlets.[50] The amount of material was simply far in excess of any readiness to assimilate it among the newspapers or their readers.

There were several contributory reasons for the failure of Durham's proposals to attract public interest – the excitement caused by *The Times'* publication, the coincidence of Glenelg's resignation, and the fact that the Report was only one of a number of publications on Canada appearing at the time. These are contributory reasons, but the main explanation for its poor reception must none the less be traced again to the disastrous mission. Durham had so much discredited himself through his own behaviour that no one was prepared to give serious consideration to his recommendations. The most telling evidence of this is to be found in his private papers or rather the evidence one would expect for a contrary view is found to be lacking. According to the *Calendar* of the Durham Papers in the Public Archives of Canada – a selection of the papers at Lambton, and presented to the Public Archives because of their relevance to Canada – only three men of any consequence wrote to Durham about his Report.[51] One was the American, Charles Sumner, who expressed his gratitude for the favourable allusions to the United States. Not only must this letter be disregarded as evidence bearing on the reception of the Report in Britain, but the grounds for Sumner's admiration were emphatically not shared by many Englishmen. A second correspondent was an old friend, Edward Bulwer Lytton. Lytton, a novelist, was scarcely an expert on colonial affairs, but nineteen years later he was to become Colonial

---

49 Francis B. Head, *op. cit.* p. iv.
50 E.g. Robert Wilmot Horton, *Ireland and Canada; supported by Local Evidence*, London 1839, and Henry Bliss, *An Essay on the Re-Construction of Her Majesty's Government in Canada*, London 1839, were both written before and partly in anticipation of the Report. Haliburton's *A Reply to the Report of the Earl of Durham* followed, as did *Facts versus Lord Durham. Remarks on that portion of the Earl of Durham's Report, relating to Prince Edward Island*, London 1839, and *Should Lord Durham be impeached? The question considered in an appeal to the electors of the House of Commons*, London 1839. The energy of the pamphleteers seems to have been considerably in excess of the receptiveness of the public.
51 Arthur G. Doughty, *Report of the Public Archives for the Year 1923*, Ottawa 1924, gives an abstract of E. L. Bulwer (Bulwer assumed his mother's maiden name of Lytton on her death in 1843) to Durham, 36 Hertford St, 8 February 1839 and Charles Sumner to Durham, 2 Vigo St, Regent Street, 11 February 1839 at p. 200.

Secretary by accident of politics. His brief term of office was marked by his firm discouragement of Sir Edmund Head's initiative for a British North American federation as a means of resolving the political crisis of 1858.[52] In this Lytton was no doubt following Durham's insistence that constitutional matters were the preserve of the Imperial Government, but it does not make his praise for the Report that of a forward-looking enthusiast for Commonwealth. The third letter, from Durham's brother-in-law Lord Howick, proposed a number of amendments in the plan sketched by the Report.[53] Indeed, so extensive were the amendments that Wakefield and Durham acidly commented that Howick was really proposing a different scheme altogether.[54] These, it would seem, were the only letters Durham received about his Report from even remotely influential contemporaries. Perhaps there were others, perhaps letters of congratulation from friend and foe did flood in upon him, but it seems unlikely. The Durham Papers are exceptionally complete and items were carefully hoarded. In view of this it seems difficult to believe that a shoal of letters in praise of the Report could have disappeared, leaving only three items of importance, plus a few oddments such as the heartcry of a disgruntled settler.[55] The more likely explanation is more ignoble and unpalatable. Durham had so destroyed his own standing in the eyes of his contemporaries that next to none of them bothered to send even the briefest note of congratulation to the author of the Report.

Historians have acknowledged that the Report was not particularly well received at its first appearance, but even so they have not drawn full attention to the vehemence of its opponents, and the absence of rational defence or indeed of rational discussion at all. It can, of course, be argued that the failure of the Report to gain public acceptance in 1839 does not necessarily prejudice its claim to be considered as an overall charter for the colonies. It must, however, be said that its initial failure of impact was so great that it would be necessary to adduce a considerable body of evidence to prove that it recovered sufficiently to be the crucial causal factor behind the major alterations in the colonial

---

[52] Public Record Office, CO 42/614, minute by Lytton, n.d., on Head to Lytton, no. 108, Government House, Toronto, C.W., 16 August 1858, fos. 295-6 and Lytton to Head (draft), no. 55, 10 September 1858, fos. 297-300.

[53] Howick to Durham, private, War Office, 7 February 1839, in Arthur G. Doughty, *op. cit.* pp. 338-40.

[54] For Wakefield's comments, Chester W. New, *op. cit.* p. 523; for Durham's comments, John W. Cell, *British Colonial Administration in the Mid-Nineteenth Century: The Policy-Making Process*, London 1970, pp. 108-9.

[55] Arthur G. Doughty, *op. cit.* gives an abstract of James Durand to Durham, no. 35 King's Square, Gosnell Road, 3 May 1839.

relationship which took place in the following decade. Unfortunately this body of evidence does not appear to exist.

4 THE INFLUENCE OF THE REPORT ON COMMONWEALTH HISTORY

The Report has traditionally been regarded as influential in three directions – as the inspiration for the Union of the Canadas in 1840, as 'the Magna Carta of colonial self-government' and to a certain extent also as prophetic of Confederation. The strongest case for immediate influence can be made out for the first of these three, while the second is of greatest concern for the Empire as a whole.

Before examining the particular there is, however, a case for looking at the general assumption that there is a necessary connection between official reports and government action. The assumption is a convenient one, but it has to be recognised that in modern times, when the machinery of government has been geared to action on a far larger scale than in Melbourne's day, many official reports have gone totally unheeded. Certainly the notion that Melbourne's government appointed a commissioner in 1838, received his Report in 1839 and acted on it in 1840, all as a conscious and intentional series of actions, would seem to attribute more vision and fixity of purpose than that government of week-to-week really deserved. In colonial matters at least, politicians seem to have been little influenced by weighty reports. In the late eighteen-forties Stephen wished to enlarge and re-organise the Colonial Office precisely so that it might produce detailed reports on the colonies, and thus turn itself into an intelligent policy-making body rather than a department administering by rule of thumb. Russell vetoed the scheme, arguing that Stephen did not 'know how little the contents of a report, or of a blue book will influence the H. of Commons. What is said in debate has far more effect.' And Russell was able to give examples of good or bad speeches which had swayed debates on colonial subjects.[1] Of course, the material for the effective speech would probably be drawn from reports and blue books, but here we are at one remove from the original. The point too can be made again that Durham was far from being the only contributor to the discussion on Canada in official and unofficial publications. What is clear is Russell's belief that a government could not get its measures

---

[1] University of Durham, Grey Papers, Stephen to Grey, 11 Avenue Fortunée, Champs Elysées, Paris, 10 November 1847, and Memorandum, 12 October 1849 in Colonial Papers; Russell to Grey, Pembroke Lodge, 24 September 1849.

through the Commons simply by reference to official reports. Measures had to be justified in terms of first principles, and could well have originated in the same way.

(*a*) *The Union of the Canadas.* The Union of the Canadas is best considered first, since it occurred first in time and since here the strongest case for Durham's influence can be made out. Durham proposed the Union of the provinces in 1839, and they were united by the Act of 1840. Closely examined, there seems to be no evidence of a causal, as distinct from a coincidental connection.[2] The Whig Cabinet which accepted the principle of Union seems to have based its decision on other proposals, without apparent reference to Durham, and it can be further argued that there was no real alternative to their decision in practical politics. When the Union came, the two Canadas were joined with an artificially equal representation. This has been regarded as a minor deviation from Durham's plan. In fact it was not at all minor — rather it reflected opposed Whig and radical views of the nature of representation. Far from being evidence of a minor amendment to a master plan, it really shows that the Whigs had arrived at the same basic solution by travelling along a very different road.

The idea of Canadian Union was an old one. The Provinces had been divided only in 1791, and in 1822 the Liverpool Government had attempted to re-unite them. A bill to create a Union was introduced into Parliament too late in the session to pass, and the matter was dropped.[3] There is evidence that at least one leading politician, Stanley, became convinced of the ultimate necessity of Union from that time onward.[4] Certainly it remained a favourite project of the English minority of Lower Canada, one of whom urged it in a letter to *The Times* in February 1837.[5] Union of the Provinces was considered by the Gosford Commission and rejected, apparently because it would meet with French Canadian opposition.[6] But French opposition ceased

---

[2] Cf. Chester W. New, *op. cit.* p. 523. 'Lord Durham's Report won its first public victory with the announcement to Parliament on May 3 that the Government would introduce legislation to effect a Union of Upper and Lower Canada.' No evidence is put forward to support the claim that it was Durham's victory.

[3] *Hansard's Parliamentary Debates*, 2nd series, VII, 20 June 1822, col. 1199; 18 July 1822, cols. 1698-1714; 23 July 1822, cols. 1729-31.

[4] *Hansard's Parliamentary Debates*, 3rd series, LIV, 12 June 1840, cols. 1137-43, and Public Archives of Canada, Derby Papers, microfilm A-31, John Richardson to Edward Ellice, duplicate, Montreal, 31 December 1822; Stanley to Spring Rice, copy, n.p. [10 June 1825].

[5] *The Times*, 16 February 1837, from 'A British Subject'.

[6] Parliamentary Papers, 1837, XXIV, p. 93 (Second Report, 12 March 1836).

to count for much after the rebellion, and as soon as news of the revolt arrived in London, the press began to give favourable consideration to Union. The *Morning Chronicle* was sympathetic, the *Morning Post* enthusiastic. The *Sun* blamed Pitt for dividing the Canadas in the first place. *The Times* and the *Examiner* both felt that Union was the only sequel to the Durham mission.[7] Consequently when the Report appeared in 1839, several newspapers were able to note quite truthfully that they had long supported Union.[8]

In October 1838 the *Globe* reported that Durham was working on a plan for a federation of all the colonies. When the *Morning Chronicle* ridiculed the report, *The Times* noted that this was 'natural enough, because all the world knows extremely well that Mr Edward Ellice patronizes a fusion of the *two* provinces of Upper Canada and Lower'.[9] In strict truth, Ellice does not seem to have reached a definite decision in favour of Union in October, but he made it clear that he was not averse to the plan, which he had worked for as far back as 1822.[10] 'Durham & Ellice have both of them the fault of thinking that all is to be done by newspapers', commented Russell, who could think of nothing 'more absurd than a Governor & his intimate friend firing paragraphs at each other across the Atlantic'.[11] Absurd or not, Ellice, Durham's 'intimate friend', was to be the real force behind the principle of Canadian Union.

The lack of any biography of Ellice has undoubtedly contributed to an under-estimate of his importance in Whig politics in the eighteen-thirties. Ellice himself did much to foster this impression. For a brief period he sat in the cabinet, mainly in his capacity as Whig election manager, but declined to resume office in 1835. He remained a powerful force and his colleagues felt his loss: Russell in 1838 wished to have him made Chancellor of the Exchequer — a senior post. What was more important was that Ellice was one of the best-informed men available on British North American affairs, largely because of his long connection with the fur trade. When the news of Durham's resignation

7 *Morning Chronicle*, 25 December 1837, 1 January 1838; *Morning Post*, 23 December, 26 December 1837; *Sun*, 18 January 1838; *The Times*, 18 January 1838; *Examiner*, no. 1564, 21 January 1838, pp. 32-3.
8 *Morning Chronicle*, 11 February 1839; *Globe*, 9 February 1839; *Morning Herald*, 9 February 1839.
9 *Globe*, 8 October 1838; *Morning Chronicle*, 17 October 1838; *The Times*, 18 October 1838.
10 Ellice to Melbourne, n.p., n.d. [October 1838], in Lloyd C. Sanders, editor, *op. cit.* pp. 438-9.
11 Public Record Office, Russell Papers, PRO 30/22/3B, Russell to Melbourne (copy), Brighton, 23 October 1838, fos. 724-5.

arrived in England, Russell advised Melbourne to 'send for Ellice directly & consult with him as to what is to be done'.[12]

In January 1838 Ellice had favoured splitting up Lower Canada —
'pray recollect "divide et impera" as the most applicable principle to
the case of these Canadians'. His plan then was close to that put forward by Sir Charles Grey at the time of the Gosford Commission:
create a separate province around the English-dominated Eastern Town-
ships, and make Quebec and Montreal free cities. At this stage the
eventual union he foresaw was not so much among the colonies, as with
remnants of a divided American Union. The most the Government
could hope for was 'to protract our dominion a little longer. . .'.[13] But
even at this stage he contemplated a straight union of the provinces as a
possibility.[14] By October he was more sympathetic to a straight union,
'a measure which, as I quite suggested it years ago, I cannot be sup-
posed to be opposed to in principle, although I fear that, without time
and preparation, it might be found both unjust and unpracticable'.[15] By
December that objection had been finally removed by the second
revolt, in which Ellice's son fell into the hands of the insurgents. By
December Ellice was definitely working for Canadian Union, and actively working against Buller's pleas for a renewed attempt at federation.[16]
Ellice's advocacy probably played a significant role in weaning Durham
away from the federal scheme, against which Ellice had fired his paragraphs.

Ellice's behaviour throughout the following months was an interesting example of self-effacement hand in hand with great influence. In
December he had been formally approached by Russell with a request
that he write a paper giving his ideas on Canada either to Melbourne or
Glenelg. He replied that he would wait for Durham's proposals to
appear, and hoped to be able to support them.[17] In short, he intended

---

12 *Ibid.* Russell to Melbourne (copy), Brighton, 18 October 1838, fos. 715-16; J.
A. Hamilton, 'Edward Ellice', *Dictionary of National Biography*, XVII, pp.
246-7.
13 Public Record Office, Russell Papers, PRO 30/22/3A, Memorandum by Ellice,
Holkham, 7 January 1838, fos. 40-2. For Sir Charles Grey's plan, see Parliamentary Papers, 1837, XXIV, pp. 246-8, 17 November 1836.
14 University of Durham, Grey Papers, Ellice to Howick, private, Holkham, 5
January [1838] and same to same, private, Holkham [7 January 1838].
15 Ellice to Melbourne, n.p., n.d. [October 1838], in Lloyd C. Sanders, editor,
op. cit. pp. 438-9. Ellice was evidently influenced by a letter from Buller
which stigmatised a Union of the Canadas as 'impossible' and 'iniquitous'.
(National Library of Scotland, Ellice Papers, E5, Buller to Ellice, Quebec, 29
September 1838, fos. 16-21.)
16 Ellice to Durham, 30 December 1838 and same to same [January 1838] in
Chester W. New, *op. cit.* pp. 488-9.
17 *Ibid.*

to wield his own influence in order to rehabilitate Durham. On 5 January 1839 he explained his intentions to Lady Howick. 'Mr Ellice who blames him really as much as we do is ready to sacrifice the Govt. methinks in order to raise Ld D out of ye mire in which he has plunged *himself.* There must be some charm in him which I have never discovered.'[18] Only after the Report had appeared did Ellice send to Melbourne his own plan for Union, feeling able to submit a scheme dated 21 December 1838 'now Durham has paved the way by giving his report. . . .'.[19] The enigmatic 'Bear' Ellice was attempting to engineer Durham's rehabilitation by giving him all the credit for a plan which had been widely attributed to Ellice in 1822, and which he had at least helped persuade Durham adopt in his Report. It was a generous act of friendship.

The Cabinet now had before them two plans for a Union of the Canadas — for Ellice's was rapidly put into confidential print. They are worth comparing. Durham gave long and detailed reasons for his recommendation, and although the case was not a novel one, he deserves the credit for a comprehensive account.[20] On the other hand, he had little to say about the mechanics of Union, contenting himself with a simple and almost abrupt recommendation of the principle. In a letter to Lord Normanby, again privately printed for the Cabinet, Chief Justice Robinson of Upper Canada confessed that he was not clear 'whether Lord Durham means that the two provinces of Canada shall have a united *legislature* only, retaining their separate *executive governments*, as at present, or whether he would consolidate the governments as well as the legislature'.[21] Ellice's plan on the other hand assumed the acceptance of the principle, and went on to offer a detailed plan. Under Ellice's plan, the two English dominated cities, Montreal and Quebec,

---

18 University of Durham, Grey Papers, Journal of 3rd Earl Grey, C3/4, 5 January 1839 (entry by Lady Howick). Stephen once called Ellice 'the busiest of busy bodies & the cleverest' (Cambridge University Library, Diary of James Stephen, Add. MS. 7511, 15 May 1846). The most likely explanation of Ellice's behaviour is to be found in an appeal from Lady Durham to do anything possible to help. 'This is the crisis of his political fate, & not only that, but much of our private happiness may be involved in it' (National Library of Scotland, Ellice Papers, E30, Lady Durham to Ellice, Gov^t. H., Devonport (1 December 1838), fos. 151-2).

19 Ellice to Melbourne, private, Woburn Abbey, 24 February 1839, enclosing a scheme dated Arlington Street, 21 December 1838, and printed in Public Record Office, CO 880/1, Confidential Print: North America, no. 3, fos. 10-12.

20 C. P. Lucas, editor, *Lord Durham's Report*, II, p. 307 for the recommendation, and II, pp. 307-28 for his reasons.

21 Public Record Office, CO 800/1, no. 19, Robinson to Normanby, Spring Gardens' Hotel, 25 February 1839, fos. 237-42.

and the area of British settlement south-east of Montreal, were to be taken from Lower Canada to form separate districts, more for purposes of representation than administration. The united colony was to be governed by a Senate of twelve members, and a Congress of sixty-four. Half of the congressmen were to be elected by Upper Canada, two each from Montreal, Quebec and the Montreal district, and twenty-six from the trunk of Lower Canada. Here is the germ of the equal representation of Upper and Lower Canada, not a deviation of detail from Durham's master plan but coming from a totally different source. One further point 'of the greatest and highest importance' deserves to be mentioned – Ellice's plan of 21 December 1838 stressed that the Crown alone should have the power to initiate money votes. On Durham's own evidence, work on the Report had to await the return from Canada of Charles Buller, who arrived on 22 December.[22] Thus even before the Report was started, one important recommendation was ready for submission to the Government from an influential source.

From the diary of Howick, who opposed the plans of both of his relatives, it appears that Ellice's scheme for Canada Union was the more influential. The cabinet met on 23 March 1839 at Lord Lansdowne's house because its owner was immobilised by gout, and there was 'some talk about Canada'. The following day the Cabinet met there again, reinforced by the presence of Labouchere, the Parliamentary Under-Secretary for Colonies, and Stephen, the Permanent Under-Secretary, 'We had a great deal of talk & it was last settled that the heads of a bill mainly founded on Ellice's project shd be prepared.' But four days later the Cabinet reversed its decision in order to consider a revised scheme by Russell. On 30 March 1839 the Cabinet had another long meeting, and discussed the rival plans of Russell and Howick. Russell was for Union, Howick merely for creating a joint commission through which the two Canadas could negotiate either a federal or legislative union if and as they wished. The Cabinet split seven against seven, but Spring Rice broke the deadlock by changing from Howick's side to Russell's. Howick, who was in the thick of moving house, had to hurry away from the Cabinet and that left the issue pretty much decided in favour of Union, although Melbourne continued to feel qualms about imposing a settlement on the French.[23]

---

[22] Public Record Office, CO 42/284, Durham to Glenelg, Cleveland Row, 20 December 1838, fo. 432.

[23] University of Durham, Grey Papers, Journal of 3rd Earl Grey, C3/4, 23 March, 24 March, 28 March, 30 March 1839; Melbourne to Russell, Panshanger, 2 April 1839; Melbourne to Russell, Panshanger, 2 April 1839 in Lloyd C. Sanders, editor, *op. cit.* pp. 444-5.

Russell's revised plan bears a strong resemblance to Sir Charles Grey's scheme for Lower Canada, put forward in 1836. The United Province of Canada was to be divided into five administrative districts, each sending twenty representatives to a General Assembly. The principle of equal representation was to be maintained at all times. This, then, was the scheme of the Canada Bill of 1839.[24] It was not to prove workable. From Canada Sir John Colborne reported that a majority in Upper Canada would support Union, but he recommended the withdrawal of all clauses likely to provoke controversy. 'The Scheme of forming new Districts and Electoral Divisions, I am persuaded, would create difficulties and embarrassments.' Colborne instead proposed the division of a number of Upper Canada counties, and the creation of two new counties in the English-speaking areas of Lower Canada. In Colborne's opinion these simple alterations would provoke little opposition, and would give each province forty-two members in the united legislature.[25] Colborne was not highly regarded by the Whigs,[26] but when supported by Poulett Thomson, the former Cabinet minister who succeeded him, the Colborne plan was to override all others. Thomson laid stress on the inequalities which would be created and the difficulty of justifying a new principle of representation. The importance of this despatch can be seen in that it was printed for the use of the Cabinet. Russell accepted Thomson's arguments, and the bill of 1840 was one substantially re-written by Thomson in Canada.[27]

Throughout these moves, there was no reference to Durham. In his confidential despatch of 24 December 1839, Thomson did ascribe to him the idea of retaining to the Crown the initiation of money votes. But in the various schemes of Union put forward, it is the influence of Ellice, Sir Charles Grey, Colborne, Howick, Russell and Thomson which can be discerned. The influence of Durham is much harder to discover. In fact, the evidence suggests a continued complete rejection of Durham by the Ministers. Robinson's letter to Normanby, for instance, criticising the Report, was deliberately withheld from Durham by the

---

24 Public Record Office, Russell Papers, PRO 30/22/3C, Memorandum on Canada, 28 March 1839, fos. 998-1001; apparently the undated 'Heads of a Bill for the future Government of the Canadian Provinces', confidential, in CO 880/1, no. 1, fos. 2-7.

25 Public Record Office, CO 42/296, Colborne to Normanby, no. 107, Government House, Montreal, 19 August 1839, fos. 46-53.

26 British Museum, Peel Papers, Add. MS. 40467, Stanley to Peel, Knowsley, 19 July 1841, fos. 35-6.

27 Public Record Office, CO 42/298, Thomson to Russell, confidential, Toronto, 24 December 1839, fos. 167-89, printed in CO 880/1, no. 8, fos. 98-100; CO 42/298, Russell to Thomson, copy, confidential, 4 February 1840, fos. 190-1; CO 880/1, no. 8, a draft bill showing alterations proposed by Thomson, fos. 121-32.

Cabinet, on the grounds that it would immediately appear in *The Times* if sent to him. It is scarcely evidence of a desire to have Durham's weighty opinion clarified. When the principle of Union had finally been accepted by the Cabinet, Normanby asked permission to tell Durham what had been decided. Durham, he said, had told him that after giving the Government his Report, he would feel badly treated if he was not told their decision. The rest of the Cabinet declined to authorise any communication, Melbourne apparently speaking for all when he said 'you will remember that all he may know he will make use of agst us'.[28] When the Ministers accepted the principle of Union, they accepted it on the basis of a plan put forward by Ellice.[29] When it came to settling details, they delved around for schemes of their own. At no point does it appear that even in the privacy of the Cabinet, ministers were investing Durham's bald recommendation of Union with any oracular status.

In public the Ministers were anxious to disclaim any connection between their policy and the Durham Report. They rested their case on the simple but inescapable conclusion that there really was no practical alternative to the Union of the Canadas. When Russell introduced the first Canada Bill into the Commons in June 1839, he went out of his way to show that Durham was not the source of the Government's inspiration, damning the Report with some very faint praise. He began with a reference to the mission to Canada. 'He was there for no very long period, and I think considering the difficulty of the details of his administration, and the immense amount of business necessarily before him, that the attention he paid to the general state of the province shows, that if he had been able to remain for the whole time originally contemplated, we should have received from him a very detailed and satisfactory account of measures by which the evils of Lower Canada could have been remedied.' The use of the conditionals is instructive: Russell's clear implication was that, unfortunately, the Government had not received any such thing. 'As the matter stands', Lord John continued, 'the report of Lord Durham contains at great length, and in very forcible language, a picture of the evils of Lower Canada, a description of the sources from which those evils have been derived, and a very strong, and I hope somewhat too strongly, coloured picture of the animosities existing between the two races of the French and British in that colony.' This, of course, was one part of the Report which Lord

---

28 University of Durham, Grey Papers, Journal of 3rd Earl Grey, C3/4, 2 March, 13 April 1839.
29 Ellice was again asked for his advice in August 1839. (National Library of Scotland, Ellice Papers, E49, Russell to Ellice, B^e Crescent, 26 August 1839, fos. 39-41.)

John could profitably touch on, in order to discredit Durham's emphasis on the 'war of races'. For contemporaries were not impressed by the logical connection between Durham's picture of communal hostility and his recommendation of a union in which that hostility would presumably become all-embracing.[30] Russell went on to ask what could be done, and pointedly discussed the alternatives without reference to Durham. The truth was that for all its failings, Union in some form was the only feasible course of action. Initiatives for an overall federation of British North America had failed to get off the ground. Indefinite continuation of military rule of Lower Canada, which was popular with the less liberal Conservatives, was obnoxious to the Whigs and the colonists, and would invite trouble with the United States. In any case, it was proving very expensive. The only other possible option – the restoration of the old constitution of Lower Canada – was out of the question. Having ruled out the alternatives, Russell confessed that he was unable to find any other plan than a Union of the two Canadas.[31]

The debates on the revised bill in the summer of 1840 again showed the inescapable nature of the Union solution. Peel, for instance, accepted the measure because it was supported by Sir John Colborne (who had been created Lord Seaton). 'He was not inclined to lay great stress on the opinions of Lord Durham. . .'.[32] While the Report was cited by some speakers, it does not seem in any way to have been decisive. Charles Buller had some fun at the expense of John Pakington, a Tory opponent of Union, showing that he only cited the Report where he happened to agree with it.[33] Opponents of Union appealed to the testimony of Sir Francis Head, whose practical authority, said the *Courier*, was worth at least a thousand times that of Durham.[34] Critics of the measure evidently thought that a good way of discrediting Union was to connect it with the Durham Report, which the Earl of Hardwicke claimed 'was not a worthy document to rest legal enactments upon'.[35] Melbourne for the Government and Gladstone for the

---

[30] Criticisms on this point were made by Pakington (*Hansard's Parliamentary Debates*, 3rd series, LIV, 29 May 1840, cols. 710-24), Colquhoun (*ibid.* cols. 741-4), and Ashburton (*ibid.*, LV, 30 June 1840, cols. 259-62). Even Captain Marryat saw that the union 'will only create a conflict between the races, as opposed to each other as fire and water' and might even drive away British migrants (*A Diary in America with remarks on its institutions.* Part Second. (3 vols.) London 1839, III, pp. 177-8). See also *The Times*, 18 February 1839.

[31] *Hansard's Parliamentary Debates*, 3rd series, XLVII, 3 June 1839, cols. 1254-75.

[32] *Ibid.* LIV, 12 June 1840, cols. 1119-28, esp. col. 1124.

[33] *Ibid.* LIV, 29 May 1840, cols. 732-40.

[34] *Courier*, 1 July 1840.

[35] *Hansard's Parliamentary Debates*, 3rd series, LV, 7 July 1840, cols. 490-505.

Opposition both in effect claimed there was no alternative to Union. Gladstone condemned Durham and said 'a choice of difficulties was the only prospect open to Parliament'. Melbourne, who made a polite reference to the Report in a second reading debate in the Lords, found it necessary in the Committee stage to qualify even that harmless allusion into nothing.[36] The *Examiner* noted that never had such an important measure passed through the Commons with so little opposition. 'It was not that the measure was not open to reasonable objections, it was not that doubts might not be sensibly entertained of its ultimate success; but it was felt that, such as it was, it was the only plan practicable, that if it were rejected, no other could be substituted. . .'[37] But in the House of Lords the Union Bill ran into a storm. The Tory peers split three ways, some supporting Peel, some opposing the Union on the grounds that it would give Canada to the rebels and the French, while Lord Ellenborough advanced the counter-argument, curious in the mouth of a Tory peer, that it would be unfair to the French.[38] This split was naturally of much embarrassment to the Conservatives, but the diverse and conflicting arguments against the measure were no more than a mirror reflection of the equally diverse reasons for it. Durham evidently thought it was a means of tying Canada to the Empire. The *Leeds Mercury* welcomed it as a step to independence.[39] In Canada, Governor Thomson found that the opponents of Union all advocated different measures, most of which they admitted 'to be their aspirations rather than measures which could practically be adopted. . .'. The Canadian critics were 'unable to suggest any course except the Union by which that at which they aim, namely, constitutional Government for themselves, could be permanently and safely established'.[40] As in Canada, so in England the advocates of Union had the advantage of marching in the same direction, even if some were out of step. For in Britain the real significance of the Union was not so much in its effect on Canada as that it conveniently bolstered conventionally accepted beliefs about the supremacy of Parliament over the British Empire. The Canadian problem had long been virtually insoluble to the British because the solution which they desired, that the French Canadians should cease to be disaffected and preferably cease to be French, was beyond the reach

---

36 *Ibid.* LIV, 29 May 1840, cols. 724-32 (Gladstone); LV, 30 June 1840, cols. 227-39 and 7 July 1840, cols. 510-19 (Melbourne).

37 *Examiner*, no. 1692, 5 July 1840, pp. 417-18.

38 The debate is in *Hansard's Parliamentary Debates*, 3rd series, LV, 30 June 1840, cols. 227-72.

39 *Leeds Mercury*, 6 June 1840.

40 Public Record Office, CO 42/297, Thomson to Russell, no. 12, Government House, Montreal, 18 November, 1839, fos. 170-174b.

of legislative fiat. Union could be argued as the nearest approximation to this, and it was a measure on a scale sufficient to satisfy the appearances of parliamentary supremacy. Peel opened his speech on the third reading of the Bill in 1840 with the assertion that it was 'necessary to the honour and credit of Parliament, that something decisive should now be done for the government of the Canadas'.[41] The argument was pungently criticised by Ellenborough who noted that Union was adopted 'not because it is just, or wise, or safe, but because it is said to be necessary "to do something" '.[42] It is difficult to avoid the conclusion that if Durham had never set foot in Canada, the Provinces would still have been united.

To deny the Durham Report the credit of having inspired the Canadian Union, and to argue that Union was in any case unavoidable, is not to argue that the Report was without any influence. Within two months of his death £2,350 had been subscribed for a monument to him,[43] which demonstrates the wide following he had among the public. Many of these no doubt accepted Canadian Union because it was Durham's recommendation. All the same, their importance should not be overestimated. If there were liberals who would accept Durham's word as gospel, so too were there Tories who would abominate everything he stood for. In Parliamentary politics only Molesworth seems to have been unswervingly loyal to tne tenets of the Report;[44] Durham did not even carry all the radicals with him.

When the Union Bill was first introduced into Parliament in the summer of 1839, Durham wrote to Ellice: 'I cannot tell you how many compliments I received from all sides Tories as well as Ministerialists.'[45] From the context it is not entirely clear whether the congratulations applied to the introduction of the Union or to Durham's refusal to be drawn into squabbles about the past. It seems highly likely that it was the introduction of the Union Bill which prompted the congratulations. In March 1840, when the measure again came before Parliament, both Russell and Ellice sent notes to Durham congratulating him on the achievement of his recommendations.[46] From this it would seem reasonable to suggest that the Report was not totally without influence.

---

[41] *Hansard's Parliamentary Debates*, 3rd series, LIV, 12 June 1840, cols. 1119-28.

[42] Public Record Office, Ellenborough Papers, PRO 30/12/24/10, untitled fragment in notes on Canada.

[43] *Examiner*, no. 1703, 20 September 1840, p. 596.

[44] H. E. Egerton, editor, *Selected Speeches*, pp. 83-4.

[45] National Library of Scotland, Ellice Papers, E30, Durham to Ellice, Cleveland Row, 27 July 1839, fos. 83-4.

[46] Russell to Durham, 25 March 1840 and Ellice to Durham, 23 March 1840 in Chester W. New, *op. cit.* pp. 561-2.

Even so, it is not an argument which ought to be pushed too far. The evidence has one common element: it was all addressed directly to Durham himself. By the summer of 1839 he had virtually ceased to be a power in politics,[47] and his Parliamentary colleagues did themselves no harm in referring politely to the adoption of his basic recommendation. In congratulating Durham on the achievement of his policy they were by no means saying that they would vote for it because it was his policy. By the spring of 1840 Durham was seriously ill,[48] and it should be remembered that the congratulations of Russell and Ellice were those of old friends to a sick man. Both men had based their advocacy of Union on other sources. The private courtesies should not obscure the public realities. Supporters of Union felt obliged to repudiate the Durham Report, while opponents of the measure attacked it as Durham's idea. There may well have been individual exceptions, but overall it seems that far from determining that the Canadas should be united, or constituting a powerful factor in the case, the Durham Report was an embarrassment.

(b) *Colonial self-government.*[49] The most important and far-reaching claims made on behalf of the Durham Report relate to its influence on the development of colonial self-government. A criticism of these claims can be reduced to three propositions. Durham did not invent the idea of colonial self-government, the form of self-government which he recommended was restricted and unworkable, and the form of self-government introduced by Grey in 1847 bore only a general relationship to the ideas of Durham.

There is really very little to say about the first proposition. It is admitted on all sides that various forms of responsible government had

---

[47] See his obituary in the *Spectator*, no. 631, 1 August 1840, pp. 732-3. 'The announcement of Lord Durham's death, although unexpected, has excited a less lively emotion than it would have done some years ago. His protracted ill-health may have had a share in this: he was probably looked upon as permanently withdrawn from the active business of life.' The *Spectator* regarded him as a leader who had refused to lead, constantly rousing hopes and then dashing them. 'Even before his illness assumed the character of permanence, disappointment had begun to predominate.'

[48] Chester W. New, *op. cit.* pp. 561-4.

[49] 'Certainly no historian ought to be as complacent about the relationship between the Durham Report and responsible government as many historians have been in the past.' (R. S. Neale, 'Roebuck's Constitution and the Durham proposals', p. 579.) Professor Neale's article appeared after the completion of this section. He demonstrated that alternative and, in his opinion, better schemes of colonial self-government existed, and that it was not possible to assume a simple causal connection between the Durham Report and everything which came after it.

been put forward before 1839 by the Baldwins, by Joseph Howe and by Roebuck and the English radicals. Durham did not invent the idea, and it seems a little strange that to a comparative late-comer such seminal importance should have been attributed. Of course, if the case for colonial self-government had not been made in England, and Durham had put it forward in a manner which had won public attention, then lack of novelty would become an irrelevant criticism. In fact, the subject had been extensively discussed and the Durham Report had not been well received.

It is much more relevant to an assessment of Durham's contribution to examine how far his ideas of colonial self-government could in fact be put into practice. 'Like most brilliant concepts, responsible government was deceptive in its simplicity. The hidden complication was, of course, that it would be extremely difficult for a governor appointed in London to be responsible both to his colonial legislature and to the imperial authority.'[50] Unfortunately, what a recent historian has seen as a 'hidden complication' was regarded by contemporaries rather as the central hitch. 'If the Governor General is constitutionally bound to act according to the advice of his responsible Government', Prince Albert asked in 1843, 'how is he to obey the instructions, which the Queen's Government may think it proper to send to him?'[51] Power, in short, could not be divided between rival authorities. The point was made by one of the most powerful political intellects of the century in a sentence remarkable for its power and conciseness. 'If the government of the dominant country govern the dependency, the representative body cannot substantially govern it, and conversely, if the dependency be substantially governed by the representative body, it cannot be substantially governed by the Government of the dominant country.' A self-governing dependency, in Cornewall Lewis's opinion, was a contradiction in terms.[52] Right down to the switch to free trade in 1846, the central problem of all responsible government schemes was the impossibility of reconciling local autonomy with the very real measure of central imperial control still necessary.

Durham hardly seems to have been aware of the crucial nature of the problem. 'The constitution of the form of government, – the regulation of foreign relations, and of trade with the mother country, the other British colonies, and foreign nations, – and the disposal of the public

50 Kenneth McNaught, *The Pelican History of Canada*, Harmondsworth 1969, p. 92.
51 Public Archives of Canada, Derby Papers, microfilm A-30, 4, Albert to Stanley, Claremont, 20 May 1843.
52 George Cornewall Lewis, *An Essay on the Government of Dependencies*, London 1841, pp. 295-6.

lands, are the only points on which the mother country requires a control', he wrote. 'This control is now sufficiently secured by the authority of the Imperial legislature; by the protection which the Colony derives from us against foreign enemies; by the beneficial terms which our laws secure to its trade; and by its share of the reciprocal benefits which would be conferred by a wise system of colonization. A perfect subordination, on the part of the Colony, on these points, is secured by the advantages which it finds in the continuance of the connexion with the Empire.'[53] In 128 words Durham disposed of the problem of dual authority, but to dispose of a problem is not necessarily to solve it.

Durham's reserved topics were open to criticism on two main fronts. First, there was the problem of defining them. This applied in particular to foreign affairs. It might be argued that the autonomy of a colony was to be limited to affairs within its own boundaries, leaving all matters outside those boundaries to the control of the imperial government. Unfortunately, quite apart from anything else, the boundary between the colonies and the United States was in dispute in several places. In 1835 there had been a minor international incident in the Indian Stream Country, which was jointly claimed by Lower Canada and New Hampshire. A Canadian law enforcement officer had been shot while trying to arrest a man in, to Canadians, his internal police work.[54] An even larger area in dispute was the upper St John valley, jointly claimed by Maine and New Brunswick. At the very moment when the Report appeared, the forces of both sides were carrying on a shadow campaign against each other deep in the Aroostook woods. It was an unpropitious moment to propose an increased measure of colonial autonomy to a British Government, which was trying without success to restrain the excitable Lieutenant-Governor, Sir John Harvey, who was being swept along by the bellicose fervour of the New Brunswickers. Harvey even justified his conduct by reporting that he had the support of his Executive Council.[55] If this was the kind of thing that could happen when the Governor was not formally bound to act on the advice of his Executive Council, it is understandable that a British

---

[53] C. P. Lucas, editor, *Lord Durham's Report*, II, p. 282.

[54] The correspondence is given in William R. Manning, editor, *Diplomatic Correspondence of the United States: Canadian Relations 1784-1860* (4 vols.), Washington, 1940-5, II, pp. 276, 289-94, 643, 974-7, 983-9; III, pp. 3-4, 8-22, 363-76.

[55] The best account of the 'Aroostook War' and of Sir John Harvey's reactions are to be found in David Lowenthal, 'The Maine Press and the Aroostook War', *Canadian Historical Review*, XXXII, 1951, pp. 315-36 and W. S. MacNutt, 'New Brunswick's Age of Harmony: the Administration of Sir John Harvey', *ibid.* pp. 105-25.

government did not wish to increase the dangers. For in Aroostook, as in Indian Stream, the colonial government could claim to be exercising no more than responsible control over its internal affairs. It was the Aroostook war which Russell referred to when he called the responsible government proposal 'one of the most important points contained in Lord Durham's report, and one on which I differ with him. . .'.[56]

This particular objection might seem a quibble, albeit an important one, were it not part of a larger problem of defining the scope of colonial self-government. Even if the boundaries had been rigidly defined, the colonies were simply too close to the United States to draw any firm distinction between their foreign and their internal affairs. Where firm boundaries existed, they were long and open. Sir Allan MacNab's local militia had crossed the St Lawrence to destroy the steamer *Caroline* during the rebellions. To increase the internal autonomy of the colonial government was in effect to enlarge its initiative in foreign affairs without any concomitant growth in responsibility. Any event inside Canada was liable to have foreign policy repercussions in the United States. This was shown in the rebellions by the summary execution of two American prisoners. It was to be shown again at regular intervals during the succeeding decades, with fugitive slaves, with the Galt tariff and throughout the Civil War. And Durham himself was not unaware of this. He warned that trouble might be stirred up on either side of the border, gradually heightening tension, until 'the officers of the respective governments, in despair of preserving peace, may take little care to prevent the actual commencement of war'.[57] On Durham's own evidence, the division between spheres of authority could not be maintained.

Even had the division been capable of definition, it is difficult to see how it could have been enforced. Durham wished the colonial Governor to be 'given to understand that he need count on no aid from home in any difference with the Assembly that should not directly involve the relations between the mother country and the Colony'. But if the Assembly could coerce the Governor into carrying out its wishes on a matter of internal policy, what was to prevent it from doing so in a quarrel involving a reserved topic? Durham himself had noted that the Lower Canada Assembly had 'endeavoured to disable the whole machine of Government by a general refusal of the supplies'. That Assembly had been attempting to extend its power into fields which Durham wished to reserve to the imperial authority, and he praised the

---

56 *Hansard's Parliamentary Debates*, 3rd series, XLVII, 3 June 1839, cols. 1254-75 and in *Selections from Speeches of Earl Russell 1817 to 1841 and from Despatches 1859 to 1865* (2 vols.), London 1870, II, pp. 49-74.
57 C. P. Lucas, editor, *Lord Durham's Report*, II, p. 271.

Legislative Council of Lower Canada for its resistance to these attempts.[58] If the Canadas were to be united, as Durham assumed, then it
was likely that in time their legislature would at least assert the pre-
tensions of its smaller predecessors. All representative bodies tend to
increase their power where they can, and the lack of any clear definition of the limit of imperial control would provide plenty of oppor-
tunities for conflict. When the conflict came, what would be the 'aid
from home' which would enforce imperial control of the reserved
topics? A Select Committee of the Legislative Council of Upper Canada
confessed itself 'at a loss to conceive how, in a government so independent as this is proposed to be made of England, these few points can by
any means be excluded from the controul of the local parliament — a
disagreement with the cabinet and legislature on the subject of foreign
trade, immigration, disposal of lands, or any of the excluded topics, will
just as readily induce a stoppage of the supplies, with all the consequences, as any of the questions within the range of [the] local
legislature. . .'.[59]

Durham's answer to this problem was contained in two brief sen-
tences, in which he pointed to four means by which imperial supremacy
could be maintained.[60] Of these, one, 'the authority of the Imperial
Legislature', was a meaningless phrase. If disaffected Canadians had
been susceptible to the fiat of Parliament, there would never have been
any rebellions. A second point — 'a wise system of colonization' —
evidently involved a system based on Wakefield's theory. Even Howick,
who was sympathetic to the theory but not to its author, thought the
sections of the Report dealing with land questions unsatisfactory.[61]
Indeed, it is difficult to see how the Wakefield system, which involved
introducing a steady stream of colonists while keeping land prices artificially high, could do anything but lead to friction between the colony
and Britain. In any case, it was to prove a non-starter. Thus two of
Durham's four arguments do not bear any examination. A third was
more plausible — 'the protection which the colony derives from us
against foreign enemies. . .'. Unfortunately its plausibility was reduced
each time it was put to the test. As Elgin insisted, the question to be
asked was 'why does Canada require to be defended, and against
whom? A very large number of persons in this community believe that
there is only one power from which they have anything to dread, and
that this power w^d be converted into the fastest friend, bone of their

[58] *Ibid.* II, pp. 280, 81, 82-3.
[59] H. E. Egerton and W. L. Grant, *Canadian Constitutional Development*, p. 184.
[60] C. P. Lucas, editor, *Lord Durham's Report*, II, p. 282 and see above.
[61] University of Durham, Grey Papers, Journal of 3rd Earl Grey, C3/6, 13 May
1840.

E

bone and flesh of their flesh, if the connexion with Great Britain were abandoned. . . Withdraw y^r protection from Canada, and she has it in her power to obtain the security against aggression enjoyed by Michigan or Maine. About as good security I must allow, as any which is to be obtained at the present time.'[62] Canada's connection with Britain had dangers as well as compensations. In 1864 John Rose, a leading Canadian politician, argued that in six of the seven war scares between Britain and the United States there had been no conceivable Canadian interest at stake.[63] As Elgin insisted 'Canada occupies a frontier position on the confines of the Empire. Whenever John Bull & Jonathan quarrel, be it on the subject of orders in Council, or of free British niggers put in gaol at Charleston, & sold to pay the expense of their keep, or of the proper policy to be pursued in Ireland, or of fisheries, or of Oregon boundaries, the shock is first felt in Canada.'[64] Of course, a strong counter-argument could be made. The presence of a British garrison in Canada no doubt constituted a deterrent to sudden attack, at least until the Civil War. Even this had its dangers for Canada: as late as 1862 the myth of effective British protection played its part in the defeat of the Militia Bill. Britain's defence of Canada against the United States was not so straightforward as Durham seemed to think, and it would not necessarily continue to be so advantageous to Canada as it was in the eighteen-thirties. It was certainly fortunate that Britain engaged in no prolonged European war in the mid-nineteenth century, for Canada was unlikely to have any enemies in Europe except by association with Britain. A war with France in particular would have produced grave internal divisions in a colony whose problems had grown chiefly out of a revival in French-Canadian national feeling.[65] Thus the argument based on British defence could only be confidently used for the contingencies of peacetime. In the realities of war, far from

---

62 *The Elgin-Grey Papers*, editor Arthur G. Doughty (4 vols.), Ottawa 1937, Elgin to Grey, private, Montreal, 26 April 1848, I, pp. 144-5.

63 Viscount Bury, *Exodus of the Western Nations* (2 vols.), London 1865, II, pp. 443-4.

64 Public Archives of Canada, Elgin Papers, microfilm A-396, Elgin to Newcastle [copy], Quebec, 28 January 1853. The original letter, marked 'private' is in University of Nottingham, Department of Manuscripts, Newcastle Papers NeC 9552.

65 The war scare of 1840 sparked off talk of a French invasion of Canada, and the Duke of Newcastle continued to fear the ambitions of Napoleon III as late as 1860. (Paul Knaplund, editor, *Letters from Lord Sydenham Governor-General of Canada, 1839-1841 to Lord John Russell*, London 1931, Sydenham to Russell, private, Government House, Montreal, 12 October 1840, pp. 96-8; University of Nottingham, Department of Manuscripts, Newcastle Papers, NeC 10889, Newcastle to Palmerston [copy], Cincinnati, 30 September 1860.)

preventing any dispute over the reserved topic of foreign affairs, the defence connection might well precipitate it.

Of Durham's four arguments, only one could be relied upon to uphold imperial supremacy in any dispute with the colony – 'the beneficial terms which our laws secure to its trade. . .' Even here there were possible drawbacks. The Canadians might have wished to transfer their trading allegiance from a British to a United States system of protection, although this is unlikely. Moreover, the argument contained a fundamental weakness which was to appear in 1846. If tariff preference for Canadian produce was in Britain's economic interests, it was unlikely that Britain would wish to invoke her most effective sanction. If on the other hand, a preference for Canadian produce was not felt to be advantageous to Britain, there could be little doubt that Britain would eventually scrap it. And in 1846 she did just that. It can of course be argued that Durham cannot be criticised for not knowing in 1839 that Protection would collapse in 1846. No doubt this is true, although it is difficult to believe that Howick, already a convinced Free Trader, would have anchored a colonial policy so strongly to what many regarded as a dying system. The question of Durham's prescience is, however, irrelevant to the larger issue of the Report's significance as the *fons et origo* of future colonial self-government. Far from originating a new chapter in imperial history, the Report was one of the last events of the old. When it was written in 1839, its future scope was to be, not the entire spread of Empire history, but the seven years to the fall of Protection in 1846. These were to be seven of the unhappiest years in Anglo-Canadian relations, years which were to prove that reconciling metropolitan and colonial authority was a much harder task than Durham had allowed. As the Tories of Upper Canada said: 'The plan of the Earl of Durham is to confine the functions of the local legislatures to affairs strictly colonial, but this limitation of powers is not practicable under his Lordship's system.'[66]

It may be objected that this criticism of Durham is irrelevant, because responsible government was introduced in the late eighteen-forties, and it was possible to reconcile imperial supremacy and colonial autonomy. This is to ignore the fact that the Elgin-Grey form of colonial self-government was much less restricted than that contemplated by Durham. It is too often and too easily assumed that Durham wished to ascribe to the imperial authority no more than the nominal suzerainty which the evolution of responsible government was ultimately to leave to it.[67] It should be noted, as Sir Charles Lucas pointed

---

66 H. E. Egerton and W. L. Grant, *op. cit.* p. 180.

67 E.g. R. Coupland, editor, *op. cit.* p. iii. 'The present status of the Dominions has been its almost automatic outcome', and L. S. Amery in *Hansard's Parlia-*

out, 'how very limited were the powers which Lord Durham proposed to give to the colonies under responsible government. . .'.[68] Two of the four reserved areas — public lands and tariffs — would have amounted to a substantial invasion of a colonial Assembly's fiscal control, assuming that imperial supremacy over them could be maintained. All colonial societies were strongly opposed to direct taxation, and a fair proportion of revenue was derived from land sales and tariffs. Attempts to defend these reserved areas would have been a formula for a continuation of the constitutional struggle fought out in Lower Canada. Durham's scheme was a long way from Dominion status.

The Grey-Elgin form of colonial self-government avoided any formal attempt at a division of powers, and so evaded the problems inherent in the Durham Report while providing a much broader scope for colonial autonomy. In the despatch to Sir John Harvey which authorised the formation of the first 'responsible government' ministry in Nova Scotia, Grey refrained from any attempt to define the areas of policy within which the new administration would be allowed to operate.[69] When Molesworth urged a Royal Commission to determine the limits of colonial and imperial authority, the Ministers resisted.[70] One by one the subjects which Durham had wished to reserve to Britain fell under effective colonial control. Parliament abandoned its control over the Clergy Reserves in 1853 — the only surviving attempt at imperial control over land granting. In 1854 Canada adopted an elective upper chamber, and cemented effective — although not legal — control over

mentary Debates, 5th series, Commons, CCLIX, 20 November 1931, col. 1199. Gerald M. Craig (ed., *op. cit.* p. vii) has claimed 'there is no reason to think that he would not have welcomed gradual devolution as colonial legislatures and governments became more competent and more experienced under the schooling that responsible government would bring'. What Durham would or would not have accepted in later years seems a profitless speculation. The most that can be suggested is that at the time of the Reform Bill he had shown no desire to support half measures which might later be extended.

68 C. P. Lucas, editor, *Lord Durham's Report*, II, p. 282n.
69 Grey to Harvey, Downing Street, 31 March 1847, in W. P. M. Kennedy, editor, *Statutes, Treaties and Documents of the Canadian Constitution 1713-1929*, 2nd ed., Oxford 1930, pp. 496-500.
70 *Hansard's Parliamentary Debates*, 3rd series, CVI, 26 June 1849, cols. 937-1004. Grey and Stephen wished to resist any enquiry into the relations between Britain and the self-governing colonies. Hawes, Parliamentary Under-Secretary for Colonies, wished to resist it only if it was put forward as an anti-government motion. Lewis, at the Home Office but author of the *Essay on the Government of Dependencies* was strongly for any enquiry. In the end Molesworth as usual overstated his case and his criticisms rebounded. (Public Record Office, Russell Papers, PRO 30/22/7F, Grey to Russell, Datchet, 29 May 1849, fos. 2183-4; University of Durham, Grey Papers, Russell to Grey, Pembroke Lodge, 24 September 1849.)

its own constitution during Confederation. In each of the first two instances action was preceded by enabling acts from Britain, but in each case it was clear that Britain had very little alternative. Nominal British supremacy was preserved in the Reciprocity Treaty of 1854, negotiated for the colonies with the United States by a special envoy. It could not escape notice that the special envoy was also Governor-General of Canada. After 1846 the colonies were effectively conceded the right to fix their own tariffs. In 1849 Canada adopted a tariff which by any objective standard would have been called Protectionist. Grey, however, accepted the face-saving plea that the intention was purely to raise revenue. A decade later the Galt tariff had to be accepted in the same way.[71] Thus subsequent events showed that Durham's formal and mechanical division of powers could not be sustained. Under Grey's system, the problems were left to solve themselves: the imperial government never abandoned its overall control in principle, but rarely if ever exercised it in practice. Significantly Cornewall Lewis, who in 1841 had called a self-governing colony a contradiction in terms, by 1849 believed that responsible government could be made to work, provided that 'people in this country see that, pro tanto, it is a concession of virtual independence to the colony'. This is a far cry from Durham's ideas, which Wakefield referred to as 'municipal self-government'.[72]

The policy of Elgin and Grey was not however one of simple surrender. Grey was opposed to formal interference in 'the internal affairs of what is now becoming more a nation than a Province'[73] but believed that much might be done through the informal influence. In 1837 he had wished to take the first steps towards a British North American federation in order to 'enable the Home Government gradually to relax the reins of its authority and to substitute a system of ruling by influence for one of direct controul'.[74] Nine years later, Stephen, a disillusioned man on the verge of retirement, argued that the British government should not bother to use its veto on unsound colonial legislation, since it would be more effective for the colonists to learn

---

71 Public Record Office, CO 42/558, Grey to Elgin (draft), no. 426, 11 October 1849, fos. 220-1, addition in Grey's handwriting; H. E. Egerton and W. L. Grant, *op. cit.* pp. 348-51.

72 Gilbert F. Lewis, editor, *Letters of the Right Hon. Sir George Cornewall Lewis, Bart. to various friends*, London 1870, Lewis to Edmund Head, Kent House, 5 April 1849, pp. 201-4; [E. G. Wakefield], *A View of the Art of Colonization*, London 1849, p. 224 and *passim.*

73 Public Record Office, CO 42/551, Elgin to Grey, confidential, Government House, Montreal, 1 June 1848, fos. 1-9, minute by Grey, 28 June 1848, fo. 13.

74 University of Durham, Grey Papers, Colonial Papers no. 100, Paper on Canada, 29 December 1837.

their mistakes from experience. Grey disagreed, arguing 'that with the greatest advantage to Canada herself this country may exercise somewhat more *influence* upon her legislat^n than Mr Stephen seems to think. . .'.[75] It was through 'a judicious use of the influence of his office, rather than of its authority' that the colonial Governor was to embody in himself the element of imperial supervision.[76] In Elgin, Grey had the ideal partner, who stoutly insisted: 'You must not however infer from my frank acceptance of the consequence of constitutional Gov^t that there is any disposition on my part to surrender my legitimate influence'.[77]

This emphasis on an informal ascendancy, exercised through the personal influence of the Governor, is reminiscent of Bagehot's description of the power of the monarchy in Britain — the right to be consulted, the right to encourage and the right to warn.[78] These were not formal powers, ones which could be reduced to articles of a written constitution. They were informal and the more effective for that. The changing position of the colonial governor can best be understood by seeing that the constitutions of Britain and Canada were evolving in parallel. This view avoids the curious delusion which pictures Canada in the eighteen-forties as a political adolescent working its apprenticeship before being allowed to enjoy the full benefits of a British constitution. In fact, a body of contemporary opinion held this to be a harmful argument, believing that the only training for the exercise of self-government was the exercise of self-government.[79] Furthermore, it assumed that the British constitution was static. It was not. Bagehot's description of the monarchy in the eighteen-sixties was a description of an institution which had only recently allowed its formal powers to fall into disuse. The power of the Crown to take independent executive action declined at much the same pace in Canada and Britain. William IV was the last British monarch to turn out his Ministers because he disliked their politics — Victoria was the last sovereign to insist on a sphere of independent action when she prevented the Tories from interfering with her household appointments in 1839. The last event of the old régime in Canada was the resignation of the Baldwin-LaFontaine

---

75 Public Record Office, CO 42/536, Trevelyan to Stephen, Treasury Chambers, 21 November 1846, and minutes by Stephen, 26 November 1846, and Grey, 28 November 1846, pp. 157-64.

76 Earl Grey, *Parliamentary Government considered with reference to Reform*, London 1864 ed., pp. 342-3.

77 *Elgin-Grey Papers*, Elgin to Grey, private, Montreal, 27 March 1848, I, pp. 139-40.

78 Walter Bagehot, *The English Constitution*, ed. R. H. S. Crossman, London 1963, p. 111.

79 E.g. *The Times*, 5 February 1849; *Morning Chronicle*, 19 March 1849.

government in December 1843 after Sir Charles Metcalfe had refused to yield up full disposal of patronage to his Ministers.[80] 1843 in Canada was an exact transcript of 1839 in England; it was Canada's Bedchamber Crisis. On each occasion the point at issue was whether or not the Crown could exercise any significant portion of its patronage independently of ministerial advice. In each case it was to be the last occasion on which the Crown exercised formal and independent power. The few later exceptions − refusals to dissolve the legislature − only harmed the overall position of the Crown's representative.[81] For most practical purposes the Crown had lost any field of independent executive action in the two largest countries of the Empire by the end of the eighteen-forties. Yet Durham's form of self-government hinged on a wide field of Crown autonomy based on enumerated powers. In essence it was a backward-looking idea. Indeed Sir Charles Metcalfe thought his course of action was thoroughly consistent with the Durham Report. 'Lord Durham advocated the system of responsible Government, which more or less must be the system of all Governments, and especially of all, of which a popular representative body forms a part.' Yet in the same despatch he confirmed to Stanley that he would insist on controlling patronage independently of his ministers.[82] Metcalfe may have misunderstood the Report, as a subsequent historian insisted, and as Stanley evidently felt at the time.[83] It is more significant that Wakefield appeared as an energetic though unwanted partisan of Metcalfe, insisting that true responsible government required an independent exercise of Crown patronage.[84] This was a very different theory from the one on which Grey and Elgin built their system. Elgin's own comment on

---

80 Metcalfe's account is in Public Record Office, CO 42/509, Metcalfe to Stanley, no. 144, Government House, Kingston, 11 December 1843, fos. 252-67.

81 This was true of Sir Edmund Head's refusal to dissolve in the Province of Canada in 1858, and especially so of Lord Byng's refusal to Mackenzie King in 1926 since he was almost immediately obliged to grant the same request to Arthur Meighen, the minority party leader. On the other hand Lord Mulgrave successfully refused a dissolution in Nova Scotia in 1859 as did Sir Patrick Duncan in South Africa in 1939. Although both the Balfour Report of 1926 and the Statute of Westminster of 1931 arose in part out of King's dispute with Byng, neither affected the power of the Crown to refuse a dissolution of Parliament.

82 Public Record Office, CO 537/142, Metcalfe to Stanley, confidential, no. 1, Kingston, 24 April 1843, fos. 6-25.

83 J. C. Dent, *The Last Forty Years: Canada since the Union of 1841* (2 vols.), Toronto 1881, I, pp. 302-3; Public Record Office, CO 537/141, Stanley to Metcalfe, copy, private, Downing Street, 29 May 1843, fos. 5-20. The draft of this despatch is in CO 537/142, fos. 26-42.

84 Public Archives of Canada, Derby Papers, A-30, 7, Metcalfe to Stanley, Kingston, Canada, 26 December 1843; [E. G. Wakefield] *A View of Sir Charles Metcalfe's Government of Canada*, London 1844, *passim*.

Sydenham's administration of Canada could equally be applied to the Durham Report: 'I never cease to marvel what study of human nature or of history led him to the conclusion that it would be possible to concede to a pushing enterprising people unencumbered by an aristocracy and dwelling in the immediate vicinity of the United States such Constitutional privileges as were conferred on Canada at the time of the Union and yet to restrict in practice their powers of self Government as he proposed.'[85]

Grey was later to compare the constitutions of the colonies before the eighteen-forties to that of Britain before 1688. The contrast is apt: Durham wished the Governor General to be Bolingbroke's Patriot King. Grey and Elgin brought the post into line with Bagehot's backstage Queen, as both Britain and Canada moved from formal to informal monarchy. Elgin evidently felt that as constitutional ruler of Canada working in harmony with the legislature through responsible ministers, he enjoyed more real power than he had possessed as the semi-autocratic ruler of Jamaica. Indeed, the old colonial constitution of Jamaica reminded him very much of its lineal descendant, the constitution of the United States. 'There is the same absence of effective responsibility in the conduct of legislation'[86] while the Elgin-Grey system brought colonial government closer to the England of Queen Victoria. Durham's scheme of a division of powers would have put them in line with the United States of Andrew Jackson. Indeed Durham actually described the United States constitution as 'a perfectly free and eminently responsible government. . .'.[87]

The contrast of Durham's scheme of 'formal' control with Grey's 'informal' system naturally calls to mind the discussion of these themes by Professors Robinson and Gallagher. The point which may be suggested here is that countries painted red on the map were not necessarily part of the empire of formal control. Indeed, in their article Robinson and Gallagher made references to Canada which suggest that they saw it as straddling the spheres of formal and informal empire.[88] In fact in Canada the maxim of Robinson and Gallagher was reversed — direct rule when possible, indirect rule when necessary. The mechanism for this informal control was political rather than economic. Nevertheless, it is an argument which may be assimilated to the theory of 'the imperialism of free trade'. Self-government in Canada was a logical and necessary consequence of Britain's abandonment of 'the beneficial

---

85 *Elgin-Grey Papers*, Elgin to Grey, secret, Montreal, 26 April 1847, I, pp. 27-9.
86 *Ibid.* Elgin to Grey, private, Toronto, 1 November 1850, II, pp. 733-4.
87 C. P. Lucas, *Lord Durham's Report*, II, p. 261.
88 J. Gallagher and R. Robinson, 'The Imperialism of Free Trade', *Economic History Review*, 2nd series, VI, 1953, pp. 1-15, esp. pp. 11, 13.

terms which our laws secure to its trade', and it is to this and not to the Durham Report that responsible government was to owe both its cause and its extent. 'The adoption of Free Trade by Great Britain, not contemplated in Lord Durham's Report, had a most powerful effect in widening the sphere of colonial self-government.'[89]

There are two possible lines of objection to the argument that the Grey-Elgin form of colonial self-government differed considerably from Durham's ideas. The first is the one which proceeds from the fact that Grey was Durham's brother-in-law, and Elgin his son-in-law, and that they were simply carrying out their relative's plan. The argument is worth examining, although its apparent assumption that ideas flow from man to man exclusively through the channel of relation by marriage can only be described as ridiculous.

It is worth examining the genesis of Grey's views on colonial self-government, since a recent historian has surmised that he was not converted to its support until after the Durham Report.[90] The only evidence which would support a view that Durham influenced Howick comes from a diary entry by the latter of a conversation about Canada in December 1837. Howick noted that 'some of his suggest[ns] were rather new to me & worth considering'.[91] There is however a considerable body of evidence in an alternative direction. Howick was the instigator of the Act of 1831, which was in line with his insistence in April 1837 that if Britain failed to get on terms with the Assembly of Lower Canada, the only alternative would be 'either endeavouring to govern the Colony by force, or of abandoning it altogether'.[92] In the immediate aftermath of the 1837 rebellion he insisted that the colony could only be governed with the support of the Assembly. He argued for an inter-colonial convention as a step towards a federation which would enable Britain to relax her authority, and persuaded Durham to adopt the idea.[93] When the Report was received by the Cabinet, Lady Howick noted that 'Henry seems to think it very able & it coincides very remarkably with his views in 33 & 34', and Howick himself observed that Russell's impressions of the Report 'seemed to correspond with what I laboured 3 & 4 years ago to impress upon the cabinet'.[94] In

89 C. P. Lucas, *Lord Durham's Report*, II, p. 282n.
90 J. W. Cell, *British Colonial Administration in the Mid-Nineteenth Century*, p. 115.
91 University of Durham, Grey Papers, Journal of 3rd Earl Grey, C3/3, 30 December 1837.
92 Public Record Office, Russell Papers, PRO 30/22/2E, Paper on Canada by Howick, 7 April 1837, fos. 1572-83.
93 *Ibid.* PRO 30/22/3A, Paper on Canada, n.d. [29 December 1837], fos. 18-29; University of Durham, Grey Papers, Colonial Papers, no. 100.
94 University of Durham, Grey Papers, Journal of 3rd Earl Grey, C3/4, 31 January, 2 February 1839.

his letter to Durham Howick's renewed argument for a federal convention went further than the autonomy contemplated by Durham.[95]
There were vicissitudes in Howick's developing thought, it is true. In
1836 he wrote 'I no longer think it would be safe to constitute a
Ministry represented in the Assembly'. He was then attracted to the
American system, under which 'the Governor like the President should
communicate with the Assembly not by choosing his servants from it's
[*sic*] Members but by Message. The responsibility which is insisted
upon has fortunately never been defined...' Under this plan, the
Assembly would have the final power through right of impeachment
before the Legislative Council.[96] The means had changed but the
general idea in Howick's mind can be traced long before Durham took
any interest in Canadian affairs. In addition Howick was one of the first
leading Whigs to support free trade, and was the only leading Whig to
object to Victoria's partisan conduct during the Bedchamber Crisis.[97] It
may be argued that if Durham had lived, and had continued to interest
himself in colonial affairs, then his ideas, like Howick's, would have
been modified by changing events. It is not, however, necessary to
adduce the Durham Report to explain the origin or development of
Howick's ideas into Grey's policy. There is even less reason to attribute
Grey's ideas to his relationship by marriage to Durham. Grey was, after
all, one of fifteen children, and in the close aristocratic circle of the
Whigs it is not surprising that he should have had extensive family
connections.

   Elgin was not appointed Governor-General of Canada because he was
Durham's son-in-law. Indeed, at the time of his appointment he was not
Durham's son-in-law.[98] Gladstone had wished to send Elgin to Canada
in succession to Metcalfe, but Elgin had not been available immediately,
and the threatening Oregon situation made it unwise to leave the post
vacant.[99] By the time Grey came into office the Oregon treaty had been

---

[95] Howick to Durham, private, War Office, 7 February 1839, in Arthur G.
Doughty, *op. cit.* pp. 338-40.

[96] University of Durham, Grey Papers, Howick to T. F. Elliot (copy), private,
War Office, 19 May 1836.

[97] Public Record Office, Russell Papers, PRO 30/22/5B, Sir Charles Wood to
Russell, private, Eaton Place, Sunday morning [July 1846], fos. 345-8 for
Grey's popularity with the Free Traders, and A. C. Benson and Lord Esher,
editors, *The Letters of Queen Victoria: a selection from Her Majesty's Corres-
pondence between the years 1837 and 1861.* (3 vols.), London 1907. Cabinet
Minute [May 1839], I, pp. 315-17.

[98] Sir Alexander Arbuthnot, 'James Bruce, Eighth Earl of Elgin', *Dictionary of
National Biography*, III, pp. 103-6.

[99] British Museum, Gladstone Papers, Add. MS. 44735, Memoranda 1845-6, list
of colonial appointments, fos. 280-5, which shows that Elgin was Gladstone's
first choice, Cathcart his fifth.

signed, and there was no reason to maintain in office the military Governor, Lord Cathcart.[100] Both in India and Canada, the Whigs took care to appoint men favoured by the Peelites,[101] and so Grey offered Canada to Elgin, whom he had never met.[102] Gladstone, who thought highly of Elgin, cordially approved of the initiative.[103] Elgin was then a widower — his first wife had died in Jamaica. He accepted Canada in August 1846. By October he had become engaged to Lady Mary Lambton, Durham's daughter and Grey's niece. In November they were married.[104] Early in January 1847 Elgin left his bride to go on ahead to Canada. Mary Elgin was not to follow until May. Elgin's first wife had died after her health had been broken in a shipwreck, and he evidently did not wish to endanger his second wife by sending her across the Atlantic in mid-winter. On arrival in Canada Elgin wrote his wife a long letter describing his inauguration as Governor-General. 'I have adopted y^r Father's view of Gov^{t}', he wrote, asking her if she remembered their vow to work together 'to build the monument which your devotion to a Parents memory made you wish to raise?' This was a natural and personal letter from a newly married man to a wife he had been forced to leave behind him. 'Did I not assure you that even when you were absent from me y^r filial affection & duty w^d animate & inspire me in the discharge of my arduous duties?'[105] For Lady Elgin had a morbid tendency to glorify dead relatives. After Elgin himself died in 1863 she was to surpass Queen Victoria in reverent widowhood.[106] In the circumstances, anything Elgin wrote to his wife in the early months of marriage should be treated with decent reserve. The notion that Elgin

---

100 *Elgin-Grey Papers*, Grey to Elgin, Belgrave Square, 4 August 1846, I, pp. 3-4.
101 Hobhouse to Russell, 14 July 1847, quoted by J. B. Conacher, 'Peel and the Peelites 1846-1850', *English Historical Review*, LXXIII, 1958, p. 441n.
102 Although Wakefield alleged in the *Spectator* (no. 1079, 3 March 1849, pp. 199-200) that Canada had been given as Lady Mary Lambton's wedding portion to a favoured nephew, there is ample evidence that the two men had never met, e.g. *Elgin-Grey Papers*, Elgin to Grey, private, Montreal, 23 April 1849, I, pp. 346-50: 'when I was appointed to Canada I had not the honor of being acquainted either with you or Lady Mary Lambton'. See also Public Archives of Canada, Elgin Papers, microfilm A-401, Elgin to Lady Elgin, n.p., Sunday [November or December 1853] and Earl Grey, *The Colonial Policy of Lord John Russell's Administration* (2 vols.), London 1853, I, pp. 208, 349.
103 University of Durham, Grey Papers, Gladstone to Grey, Fasque, Fettercairn, 13 August 1846.
104 The romance can be followed in University of Durham, Grey Papers, Journal of 3rd Earl Grey, C3/13, 6, 8 October, 7 November 1846.
105 Public Archives of Canada, Elgin Papers, microfilm A-401, Elgin to Lady Elgin, Monklands, 31 January 1847.
106 Ronald Hyam, *Elgin and Churchill at the Colonial Office 1905-1908: the watershed of the Empire-Commonwealth*, London 1968, pp. 12-13.

decided to introduce responsible government into Canada because he had fallen in love with Durham's daughter two months after being appointed Governor-General, is surely too absurd to be entertained. Much more revealing is a letter which Elgin sent to his wife in 1853 when the Duke of Newcastle was taking an inordinately long time to decide whether or not Elgin should be re-appointed for another term. 'He is actually forcing *my system* on every colony in the Empire and if he could get me out of the way he would be able all the better to claim exclusive credit for it.'[107] After seven years of marriage responsible government had become '*my system*', without reference to the father-in-law whom Elgin had probably never met.

The second line of objection would be based on the argument put forward by Charles Buller in 1840. Buller argued that 'the union of the Canadas carried responsible government with it as a necessary consequence'.[108] The province created would be too large to hold down, and so the one followed from the other. A defence of Durham would argue that the extent of the colonial self-government which was eventually introduced was irrelevant, the important point being that Durham had seen that Union necessarily involved responsible government. In support of this argument it could be pointed out that as early as 1842 Bagot concluded 'whether the doctrine of responsible Government is openly acknowledged, or is only tacitly acquiesced in, virtually it exists. . .'.[109] This argument may give Durham credit for foreseeing the need for responsible government, but it only throws into relief the impracticability of his arbitrary attempt to limit its scope. Even if this point is left aside, there remains an insuperable objection to this defence of Durham. Both Bagot and Elgin found that self-government in Canada required partnership between the British and French communities. Durham made it abundantly clear that Union was intended by him as a means of swamping and denationalising the French. Once again, Durham's sweeping conclusions had overlooked the immediate and practical problems. No doubt immigration would one day overwhelm the French, said Sir Charles Bagot, but what was he to do in the meantime if he lost his majority in legislature?[110] While the Anglo-Canadians split into factions, the French stood firm together, so that no strong government could be formed without them. The French stood together because they stood on the defensive – united against the

107 Public Archives of Canada, Elgin Papers, microfilm A-401, Elgin to Lady Elgin, n.p., Sunday [November or December 1853].
108 *Hansard's Parliamentary Debates*, 3rd series, LIV, 29 May 1840, col. 734.
109 Public Archives of Canada, Derby Papers, microfilm A-30, 6, Bagot to Stanley, private, Kingston, 28 October 1842.
110 *Ibid.* Bagot to Stanley, private, Quebec, 10 June [error for July] 1842.

Englishmen, of whom Durham was a notably unfeeling example, who made no secret of their desire to hurry the French Canadian separate identity to the grave. Thus Durham's contribution to Canadian self-government is not one which would point to the bi-cultural partnership which subsequently emerged.

On the strength of an assumed causal connection between the Report and colonial self-government, Durham had traditionally been regarded as a founder, father or godfather of the modern Common-wealth. The chronology of the introduction of responsible government alone casts doubt on this — 1847, Nova Scotia; 1848, Canada; 1856, New South Wales, New Zealand and Victoria; 1862, Queensland; 1872, the Cape; 1890, Western Australia. Responsible government, it might be said, came when colonies were large enough to manage it or strong enough to demand it.[111] It is difficult to see any point at which the Durham Report advanced the introduction of self-government into a colony by as much as twenty-four hours. Nevertheless it might be said that there is no harm in the popular myth which sees the Report as in some way a symbolic fount of a Commonwealth of self-governing nations. However, one point has been touched on which does rob Durham of any entitlement to be considered a founder of the modern Commonwealth. Self-government is one important element in the modern Commonwealth, but another is multi-racialism. Durham's atti-tude to the French and his proposed measures to assimilate them are at variance with the present day association. This is a non-historical judgement, an attempt to measure the Durham Report against twen-tieth century standards, and it stands independently of the general analysis. But when it is claimed that the Durham Report was the blue-print for self-government within the Empire, it is worth asking — self-government for whom?[112]

(*c*) *British North American Union.* The interval between the publi-cation of the Durham Report in 1839 and the achievement of Con-federation in 1867 is obviously too long for even the most enthusiastic hagiographer to argue for a causal connection between the two. The most Sir Charles Lucas would say was that 'it bore full fruit' in 1867.[113] Confederation arose out of a combination of the needs and oppor-

---

111 Cf. R. S. Neale, 'Roebuck's Constitution and the Durham proposals', esp. p. 590.

112 Professor Neale has even suggested that Durham would have supported the 1965 rebellion in Rhodesia. This kind of speculation is essentially profitless, but Europeans in Southern Rhodesia could probably appeal to the Report with greater consistency than many others (*ibid.* p. 581).

113 Introduction by Lucas to George Cornewall Lewis, *An Essay on the Govern-ment of Dependencies*, ed. C. P. Lucas, London 1891, p. xxvii.

tunities of the colonies themselves, not in obedience to precepts laid down a quarter of a century earlier. But even so, ideas can be influential in themselves, even if changes in time and circumstances are required to bring them to fruition. What then did Durham propose, how far was he original, and how far did his Report keep the idea of closer union alive until its opportunity came?

'On my first arrival in Canada, I was strongly inclined to the project of a federal union', Durham explained.[114] He went so far as assembling a convention of delegates from the colonies to discuss federation.[115] The scheme was discussed in the British Press.[116] All the signs were that Durham would recommend a federation of at least the mainland colonies of British North America. But abruptly he changed his mind. He had been aware of the theoretical objections to federal government – its weakness, and its inapplicability to colonies, 'the greater part of the ordinary functions of a federation falling within the scope of the imperial legislature and executive. . .'. Now he became aware of practical disadvantages, especially the dangers of leaving any power in the hands of the French.[117] The renewal of rebellion in the winter of 1838 almost certainly converted him under pressure from Edward Ellice from federal to legislative Union of all the colonies, of which Canadian Union was to be the first step.[118] Perhaps too, like later governors, his stay in Canada had convinced him that the colonies scarcely possessed enough political talent to fill one assembly and still less if spread across half a dozen legislatures, many of them having no very elevated functions to perform. Durham's belated change of mind was not, incidentally, commented upon much by contemporaries and it did the Report no harm. One reason for this was the widespread failure to understand what Durham was in fact proposing. Another was that the discussion of legislative Union was obviously designed to set a long-term aim, and was not of immediate relevance. John Beverley Robinson insisted that the Report was 'in effect recommending an union of the Canadas *merely*, though it may have the appearance of something more'.[119]

Once again, the significance of Durham's proposal for British North American Union can only be appreciated by setting it in context. The

---

114 C. P. Lucas, editor, *Lord Durham's Report*, II, p. 304.
115 Public Record Office, CO 42/283, Durham to Glenelg, no. 58, Castle of St Lewis, Quebec, 13 September 1838, fos. 162-3.
116 E.g. *Globe*, 8 October 1838; *Standard*, 10 October 1838; *Morning Chronicle*, 17 October 1838; *The Times*, 18 October 1838.
117 C. P. Lucas, editor, *Lord Durham's Report*, II, pp. 304-7.
118 Chester W. New, *op. cit.* pp. 485, 488-90.
119 Public Record Office, CO 880/1, Confidential Print, North America, no. 19, J. B. Robinson to Normanby, Spring Gardens' Hotel, 23 February 1839, fos. 237-42.

idea of Union was not itself a new one: Colonel Robert Morse had suggested amalgamation as early as 1784 in order to create 'a formidable rival to the American States'.[120] By 1839 there were three main schemes of Union in existence. One was colonial federation, analogous to that of the United States. It had been put forward by Robert Gourlay in 1822, and urged by Roebuck in the Commons in April 1837.[121] Buller ascribed Durham's original scheme to Roebuck, and Roebuck submitted a lengthy memorandum of his proposals.[122] The second scheme was a legislative Union of the colonies, analogous to that of the United Kingdom. Chief Justice Sewell had evidently persuaded the Duke of Kent of the wisdom of this plan as far back as 1814 − this of course was revealed by Durham himself, who made no claim to originality. The idea was revived in 1839 by Henry Bliss in a pamphlet evidently written and published before the Durham Report.[123] Bliss was the Agent for New Brunswick and acted unofficially on behalf of the Legislative Council of Lower Canada to counter Roebuck, the spokesman of the Assembly.[124] These two schemes shared a common flaw: they were both dramatic and static in conception. They were dramatic in that they required some violent catalyst to jerk the colonies out of their old ways, and static in that they assumed that once brought into being they would never require any adjustment. A wand would be waved and a colonial nation would spring fully formed into life. Durham's mind was naturally drawn to such grand conceptions, although he envisaged a federation which would eventually solidify into a much closer Union.[125] The third extant scheme, that of Howick and Stephen, took account of the tendency of constitutions to evolve along lines of their own. Popular assemblies, especially in colonies, tended to engross their powers. Therefore the two men wished to create a joint commission of the mainland colonies, with powers to co-ordinate certain matters of common interest. Gradually this might be expected

---

[120] Morse's Report on Nova Scotia, 1784, is printed in Douglas Brymner, *Report on Canadian Archives for 1884*, Ottawa 1885, pp. xxvii-lix.

[121] Robert Gourlay, *General Introduction to Statistical Account of Upper Canada compiled with a view to a grand system of Emigration in connexion with a reform of the Poor Laws*, London 1822, p. cccxxxviii; *Hansard's Parliamentary Debates*, 3rd series, XXXVII, 14 April 1837, cols. 1209-29.

[122] Buller's 'Sketch' in C. P. Lucas, editor, *Lord Durham's Report*, III, pp. 362-3; Roebuck's Letter no. III, 15 November 1838, *Spectator*, no. 541, 17 November 1838, pp. 1084-5; J. A. Roebuck, *op. cit.* pp. 193-220.

[123] C. P. Lucas, editor, *Lord Durham's Report*, II, p. 321; Henry Bliss, *An Essay on the Re-Construction of Her Majesty's Government in Canada*, London 1839.

[124] *Colonial Magazine*, IX, September-December 1846, p. 308; *The Times*, 20 January 1838, letter of 'N.G.'.

[125] C. P. Lucas, editor, *Lord Durham's Report*, II, p. 305.

to increase its powers, and the British Government might 'relax the reins of its authority' and substitute influence for domination.[126] In January 1837 the Whigs had drafted a bill to introduce this evolutionary federation.[127] Of the three possible plans for closer union, it was the least widely known, but it was influential in the official world of Stephen and Howick.

The Durham Report added nothing then that was new. Nor did it do much to keep the idea of closer union alive. Publicly the impetus came from Roebuck, privately from Howick after he had inherited his father's title and taken the seals of the Colonial Office. Roebuck in 1849 published the memorandum he had submitted to Durham, as part of his *Colonies of England*, which argued strongly for a federation of the North American Colonies.[128] He followed this with a motion in the House of Commons to the same end.[129] In the years which followed the idea was not infrequently associated with Roebuck rather than with Durham.[130]

Roebuck's public advocacy was paralleled by Grey's private encouragement. Elgin was instructed to be a real and not simply a nominal Governor-General of British North America, and to work for the establishment of a common connection amongst the provinces. Elgin, however, reported that nothing could be done; Grey accepted that communications were not good enough to make Union possible but consoled himself with the thought 'that short as the tenure of office generally is while one holds it one ought to act as if it were to be permanent or as if ones successor was likely to carry forward the policy one has begun'.[131] Two years later Russell raised the question of federation again — almost certainly as a result of Roebuck's advocacy.[132]

126 University of Durham, Grey Papers, Colonial Papers no. 100, Howick's paper of 29 December 1837; Stephen to Howick, Kensington Gore, 28 December 1837, and Colonial Paper no. 99 by Stephen of same date; Journal of 3rd Earl Grey, C3/3, 29 December 1837.

127 Public Record Office, CO 537/137, Epitome of the proposed Canada Act, 19 January 1837, fos. 196-202.

128 J. A. Roebuck, *op. cit.* pp. 193-220.

129 *Hansard's Parliamentary Debates*, 3rd series, CV, 24 May 1849, cols. 928-64.

130 E.g. *Dublin University Magazine*, XXV, February 1850, p. 167; *Daily News*, 10 July 1858.

131 Public Record Office, CO 42/534, Grey to Elgin (draft), no. 10, 31 December 1846, fos. 369-79; CO 42/541, Elgin to Grey, on board R.M.S.P. *Hibernia*, 23 January 1847, fos. 26-35; *ibid.* Elgin to Grey, confidential, Government House, Montreal, 18 February 1847, fos. 41-56; *Elgin-Grey Papers*, Elgin to Grey, private, Montreal, 7 May 1847, I, pp. 34-7; *ibid.* Grey to Elgin, private, Belgrave Square, 16 June 1847, I, pp. 47-8.

132 University of Durham, Grey Papers, Russell to Grey, Pembroke Lodge, 6 August 1849.

Elgin persuasively insisted that a legislative Union was preferable to federation and, more than ten years after Durham's presentation of the same case, Grey confessed 'I am rather coming round to your view of it. . .'.[133] No reference was made to Durham.

It is difficult to escape the conclusion that Elgin was much more interested in the immediate problem of responsible government than the academic merits of federations. In this, his successor, Sir Edmund Head, was his antithesis. Head, unlike Elgin, was a poor manager of men but an enthusiastic projector of measures. Grey's idea of a 'Zollverein' — a customs union leading to political union — was raised by him in correspondence with Elgin as early as 1848.[134] In the next decade Head was to touch on the question of closer union of some or all the colonies several times. His most detailed federal blueprint dates from 1851, an impressive memorandum six thousand words long. It contains no reference to Durham.[135] Yet Edmund Head was a 'Scholarly Governor' in the soubriquet of his biographer.[136] He, more than any other man in the colonial service, might have been expected to draw his ideas from precedent, to have based his case on the witness of great predecessors. In fact Head drew his conclusions principally from the example of the United States, and the book which had the most influence on him was Joseph Story's *On the Constitution of the United States* and not the Durham Report.[137] Head did indeed refer to the Report in his briefer memorandum of 1858, but he merely cited Durham's objections to giving Upper and Lower Canada equal representation. Although the second part of his memorandum dealt with the need for general federation, he did not bother to add that Durham had regarded the Union of the Canadas as a step to a larger Union.[138] Head's federal initiative of 1858 was to inject the issue into Canadian politics, but it failed to achieve anything itself. The reason for this failure must be sought largely in the discouragement it received from Sir Edward Bulwer

---

133 Public Record Office, Russell Papers, PRO 30/22/8A, Grey to Russell, Howick, 8 August 1849, fos. 62-5; *Elgin-Grey Papers*, Grey to Elgin, Howick, 8 August 1849, I, pp. 437-8; *ibid.* Elgin to Grey, private, Montreal, 3 September 1849, II, pp. 463-6; *ibid.* Grey to Elgin, Balmoral, 22 September 1849, II, pp. 470-1.

134 Public Archives of Canada, Elgin Papers, microfilm A-398, Head to Elgin, private, Government House, Fredericton, 27 May 1848.

135 Chester Martin, 'Sir Edmund Head's First Project of Federation, 1851', *Canadian Historical Association Annual Report for 1928*, pp. 14-26.

136 D. G. G. Kerr, *Sir Edmund Head: A Scholarly Governor*, Toronto 1954.

137 E.g. *Canadian Historical Association Annual Report for 1928*, p. 18; National Library of Wales, Harpton Court Collection, C/1516, Head to G. C. Lewis, Government House, Fredericton, 2 March 1850.

138 Chester Martin, 'Sir Edmund Head and Canadian Confederation, 1851-1858', *Canadian Historical Association Annual Report for 1929*, pp. 11-14.

Lytton at the Colonial Office.[139] And Lytton had been one of the two prominent Englishmen who had bothered in 1839 to write congratulating the author of the Durham Report.[140]

When Confederation came, it managed its work without any extensive reference to Durham. Only one colonial governor quoted from the Report in official correspondence — Arthur Gordon of New Brunswick, who objected that the Quebec scheme preserved too great a measure of autonomy to the despised assemblies of the individual provinces. He made lengthy quotations from the Report, arguing for legislative rather than federal Union. For good measure he added Elgin's opinions too. The Colonial Office, ministers and officials, reacted as they were to do to every anti-Confederation jeremiad they were to receive from the same source during the next two years — they ignored it.[141] If there was a magic chord which supplied the theme of British colonial policy, Arthur Gordon at any rate had failed to touch it with his reference to the Durham Report.

Far from the Durham Report 'causing' Confederation, it was rather true that the British North America Act gave rise to the first stirrings of the mythology which came to surround the Report.

5 THE GROWTH OF THE MYTH

The plain fact is that mid nineteenth-century colonial policy was not based on the textual criticism of the Durham Report. It was rather that after the Canadian problems it dealt with had been resolved it began to be looked back on as a landmark, and one which might contain the key to other imperial riddles. The myth of the Durham Report was a posthumous myth. There is no trace of it in the years after 1839 when the problems of Canada were in the forefront of British policy.

It is difficult to grasp just how ephemeral the document itself really was. Within a year of its appearance, Charles Buller had anonymously published his *Responsible Government in Colonies* because, he said,

---

139 Public Record Office, CO 42/614, minute by Lytton, n.d., on Head to Lytton, no. 108, Government House, Toronto, Canada West, 16 August 1858, fos. 295-6 and Lytton to Head, draft, no. 55, 10 September 1858, fos. 297-300.

140 The abstract of Bulwer to Durham, 36 Hertford St, 8 February 1839 is in A. G. Doughty, *op. cit.* p. 200.

141 Public Record Office, CO 188/141, Gordon to Cardwell, confidential, St Stephen's, New Brunswick, 11 October 1864, fos. 269-92, with formal minutes at fo. 291.

Durham's ideas had been 'often misunderstood and misrepresented'.[1] That too was ephemeral – nine years later Wakefield reprinted part of Buller's pamphlet in his own *Art of Colonization*, because the original had altogether disappeared from circulation.[2] The same process of eclipse overtook the Durham Report. In August 1840 the *Colonial Gazette*, by then a companion paper of the *Spectator* and hence a Wakefield organ, was complaining that the Report was 'well-nigh forgotten' in England.[3] Two years later T. W. C. Murdoch informed Sir Charles Bagot that anonymous articles had appeared defending his policy in the *Morning Chronicle*. 'From the knowledge of persons and things, and the allusions to Lord Durham's report, I have little doubt that these articles are written by Charles Buller.'[4] So precise an identification could hardly have been possible had the Report held a central place in public discussions of colonial affairs.

The death of Durham in July 1840 provides a useful point at which to measure the esteem in which the Report was then held in Britain. Although one periodical specifically repudiated *'de mortuis nil nisi bonum'* in its obituary,[5] it might be anticipated that assessment of Durham at his death would, where possible, incline to favourable glosses on his career, more especially since the passage of the Union Act had more or less removed Canadian affairs from the centre of British politics. A few newspapers did refer to the Report. The *Morning Chronicle* called it 'one of the most masterly and statesmanlike surveys of a country abounding in all manner of anomalies, that ever was executed'.[6] The *Leeds Mercury* made the dubious assertion that it was 'upon his bold and statesmanlike Report that the Ministerial measure for the government of Canada was formed'.[7] Both had been favourable to the Report at its first appearance, although less enthusiastic then than at his death.[8] The *Colonial Gazette* mourned the passing of the only British statesman who understood the colonies. 'Lord Durham's

1 E. M. Wrong, editor, *Charles Buller and Responsible Government*, Oxford 1926, reprints Buller's *Responsible Government for Colonies*, pp. 86-170, esp. p. 86.
2 [E. G. Wakefield], *Art of Colonization*, pp. 277-8, 279-96.
3 *Colonial Gazette*, no. 90, 12 August 1840, p. 529. The paper had been published at the *Spectator* office since 7 August 1839. For Wakefield's influence on the two papers, see [E. G. Wakefield], *Art of Colonization*, pp. 52, 59.
4 Murdoch to Bagot, 18 October 1842, in G. P. de T. Glazebrook, *Sir Charles Bagot in Canada: a study in British Colonial Government*, Oxford 1929, p. 109. The articles referred to were evidently those in the *Morning Chronicle* of 15, 17 October 1842.
5 *Colonial Magazine*, III, September 1840, pp. 60-6.
6 *Morning Chronicle*, 30 July 1840.
7 *Leeds Mercury*, 1 August 1840.
8 *Morning Chronicle*, 9 February 1839; *Leeds Mercury*, 16 February 1839.

Canadian mission will be his monument. In every colony of England his "Report on the Affairs of British North America" has been reprinted and circulated, and, we had almost said, got by heart.'[9] The *Colonial Magazine* was less enthusiastic about 'the celebrated Canadian report' which, it said, 'abounded with truisms, contained several erroneous principles, and often mistook effects for causes; but not a few just and sound ideas were promulgated, and very many valuable facts were collected and registered for public investigation, while its tone was bold and manly though too egotistical'.[10] Many of the obituary notices did not refer to the Report at all. *The Times* continued its feud beyond the grave, admitting only that some of Durham's faults 'may have proceeded more from ill-health, than from original infirmity of moral temper'.[11] In a half-column article the *Manchester Guardian* found space to mention that Durham was High Steward of Hull, but made no reference to the Canadian mission.[12] The *Spectator* referred to Canada, but not to the Report,[13] while the *Examiner* in a long leading article mentioned neither.[14] One can only conclude that the bulk of his contemporaries either thought the Report on the Affairs of British North America too unimportant to mention, or were anxious not to speak ill of the dead.

The same absence of comment can be seen in the three most comprehensive contemporary surveys of colonial policy. Cornewall Lewis in 1841 made only three brief references to the Report, an omission which Sir Charles Lucas made good with a profusion of footnotes in his 1891 edition.[15] Lucas was evidently puzzled by this anomaly, and tried to explain it away by saying that only one passage in the book referred to colonial self-government. Even so, there was no reference to the Durham Report in it.[16] The explanation was unconvincing, for Lewis's book was 'An Essay on the Government of Dependencies' and Lucas himself was to describe the Durham Report as 'a general essay upon the best method of adjusting the relations between Great Britain and British Colonies which are not merely dependencies. . .'[17] Lewis however had used the term 'dependencies' in its strict sense, and the

9 *Colonial Gazette*, no. 89, 29 July 1840, p. 503.
10 *Colonial Magazine*, III, September 1840, pp. 60-6.
11 *The Times*, 30 July 1840.
12 *Manchester Guardian*, 1 August 1840.
13 *Spectator*, no. 631, 1 August 1840, pp. 732-3.
14 *Examiner*, no. 1696, 2 August 1840, p. 481.
15 The difference between Lewis and Lucas in their appreciation of Durham is best seen in G. C. Lewis, *An Essay on the Government of Dependencies*, ed. C. P. Lucas, London 1891, footnotes *passim*.
16 *Ibid*. pp. 299-300 and footnotes.
17 C. P. Lucas, editor, *Lord Durham's Report*, I, p. 115.

contradiction could not be explained away by the adverb 'merely'. Lucas himself must have realised this, for he finally admitted that Lewis 'though he published his book in 1841, after *Lord Durham's Report* had seen the light, conceived of a colonial Empire as consisting solely of dependencies'.[18] Lewis, he had to admit, had no vision of an Empire of self-governing Dominions. In short, Cornewall Lewis had failed to see Durham's light. In the same year, Herman Merivale revised his Oxford lectures in order to refer to Lewis, but Durham did not even appear in his index.[19] Grey in 1853 made a ritual allusion to 'Lord Durham's well-known Report' but from the rest of his book it is clear that it was the fact and not the contents of the Report which merited the description he gave.[20]

During the three nights of debates on the Rebellion Losses Bill in 1849 − 'the only true parliamentary test responsible government ever received'[21] − only one man cited the Durham Report, and he, ironically enough, was Lord Brougham. And Brougham merely quoted Durham on the war of races, which Russell in 1839 had broadly hinted was highly coloured, and which was described in the *Colonial Magazine* in 1849 as 'well known in Canada' to have been 'a gross exaggeration made to give effect to the union of the provinces'.[22]

In the official records the same picture emerges − or rather the alternative fails to do so. Sydenham mentioned Durham in his despatches only to complain about the debts caused by his predecessor's free-handed spending.[23] In private correspondence with Russell he appealed only once to Durham's testimony − on a fairly technical

[18] C. P. Lucas, *Greater Rome and Greater Britain*, Oxford 1912, p. 125.
[19] H. Merivale, *Lectures on Colonization and Colonies: delivered before the University of Oxford in 1839, 1840 and 1841* (2 vols.), London 1841-2, esp. II, p. 294n. for the influence of Lewis.
[20] Grey, *Colonial Policy*, I, pp. 201-2.
[21] J. W. Cell, *op. cit.* p. 112.
[22] *Hansard's Parliamentary Debates*, 3rd series, CVI, 19 June 1849, cols. 450-83; *ibid.* XLVII, 3 June 1839, cols. 1254-75; *Colonial Magazine*, XVI, 1849, p. 452.

Brougham's quotations can be found in C. P. Lucas, editor, *Lord Durham's Report*, II, pp. 16-17, 27, 39, 45, 53, 56, 59, 60-1 and 62. References in this section to quotations from the Report are taken from the Lucas edition, as the best available complete text, although in many cases it is anachronistic.

Durham's 'war of races' picture was criticised at the time by John Neilson: 'There is, indeed, no truth in the irreconcilable hatred between the inhabitants of Canada, of British and French origin, even amongst the excitements occasioned by late events.' (*Quebec Gazette*, 29 April 1839, quoted by M.-P. Hamel, editor, *Le Rapport de Durham*, Quebec 1948, p. 46.)
[23] Public Record Office, CO 42/310, Thomson to Russell, no. 100, Government House, Montreal, 4 May 1840, fos. 37-42; CO 42/311, Sydenham to Russell, no. 171, Government House, Montreal, 6 October 1840, fos. 327-8.

aspect of Upper Canada local government.[24] Few men have used the
first person singular pronoun more than Sydenham: the idea that his
policy was merely derivative cannot be supported, although it had
greater affinity to Durham's ideas than to those of Elgin. Bagot referred
extensively to Sydenham in his private correspondence with Stanley,
but only once to Durham, when he admitted that to bring the French
into government would be 'certainly in opposition to Lord Durham's
recorded sentiments' as well as to Stanley's.[25] Bagot made it clear that
his point of departure was the policy laid down by his immediate
predecessor, and when in September 1842 he had to admit the Reformers to his Ministry he justified his course purely by a recital of
events, not by appeal to Durham.[26] The only Canadian Governor to
appeal to the Report was Metcalfe.[27] He received a cool reply from the
Colonial Secretary, and subsequent Canadian historians have been
anxious to insist that he had misunderstood the Report – a 'mistake'
which he shared with Wakefield, his unwanted supporter.[28] In the
Colonial Office the Report was entombed in the archives where it may
be seen today, its 346 folios with their fresh white margins bare of
dusty fingermarks and other signs of frequent use. A document in
frequent use in the Colonial Office would normally betray marginal
annotations and faded underlinings in pencil where permanent staff
drew the attention of their political masters to key passages. It is
possible to turn over 329 folios before finding even the slightest trace
of such marks – and then they appear in Appendix E dealing with the
lands of the Seignory of St Sulpice in Montreal.[29] Of course, this is
subjective rather than conclusive evidence. It may be that this copy,
signed as it was by Durham, was reverently preserved while the staff of
the Office made such heavy use of other copies that they may have
disintegrated from constant handling. All that can be said is that there

24 Paul Knaplund, editor, *Letters from Lord Sydenham*, Thomson to Russell,
    private, Drummondville, 28 August 1840, pp. 85-7. He also cited Durham's
    views on local government in a despatch. (Public Record Office, CO 42/311,
    Thomson to Russell, no. 160, Toronto, 16 September 1840, fos. 235-48.)
25 Public Archives of Canada, Derby Papers, microfilm A-30, 6, Bagot to Stanley,
    private and confidential, Quebec, 20 July 1842 for his reference to Durham,
    passim for discussions of Sydenham's policy.
26 *Ibid*. Bagot to Stanley, private, Kingston, 13 September 1842; same to same,
    private, Kingston, 26 September 1842.
27 Public Record Office, CO 537/142, Metcalfe to Stanley, confidential, no. 1,
    Kingston, 24 April 1843, fos. 6-25.
28 *Ibid*. CO 537/141, Stanley to Metcalfe, copy, private, Downing Street, 29 May
    1843, fos. 5-20; J. C. Dent, *The Last Forty Years*, I, pp. 302-3; [E. G.
    Wakefield] , *Sir Charles Metcalfe's Government, passim*.
29 The Report and appendices are in Public Record Office, CO 42/299, fos.
    79-423. Pencil marks may be seen on fos. 408-11.

is no supporting evidence from minuting of despatches from Canada for the next twenty-seven years that any such reference was ever made. Indeed, when Durham submitted his fourth appendix in May 1839, Stephen protested against the cost of publishing something dealing with a problem — Jesuit estates — which could only be settled in Canada, and which would therefore be 'utterly useless in this country'.[30]

Despite its overall neglect of the Report, the mid-nineteenth century did leave a few appreciative remarks on record. Charles Buller praised the Report in 1847, Harriet Martineau in 1850, and John Stuart Mill in 1859. Mill said that the Report began 'a new era in the colonial policy of nations', although he did not specify which nations.[31] They were radicals; Buller had accompanied Durham to Canada, Mill had publicly lauded the Report before it had been written.[32] Yet they provided the testimony on which later historians could build a case for its influence. Lucas in 1891 wrote that the Report 'was the beginning of a new era in the colonial policy of Great Britain'.[33] Although borrowing Mill's phrase without acknowledgement, Lucas had by implication accorded him the status of a neutral, not a partisan observer. The same quotation from Mill could in 1970 provoke the remark: 'That era has continued down to the present day and will no doubt continue to do so until the final end of British colonialism'.[34] The Report, which had once represented the salvation of the Empire, now symbolised its peaceful dissolution. That there was contemporary evidence which could be adduced in support of either argument shows how merely laudatory that evidence was. Moreover, these scattered words of praise for the Report in no sense constituted a representative judgement of contemporaries.

Nevertheless, these comments by Durham's friends do mark the first beginnings of a myth which was to flower around 1900. Their effect can be traced in the preface Merivale wrote to the 1861 edition of his *Lectures*. 'The Canadian outbreak of 1837, the consequent mission of

30 Public Record Office, CO 42/299, minute by Stephen, 27 May 1839, fo. 43, on Durham to Normanby, Cleveland Row, 25 May 1839, fos. 42-3.

31 See the last sentence of the review attributed to Buller in *Edinburgh Review*, LXXXV, 1847, pp. 358-97; Harriet Martineau, *The History of England during the Thirty Years Peace 1816-1846* (2 vols.) London 1849-50, II, pp. 391-2; J. S. Mill, *On Liberty and considerations on Representative Government*, ed. R. B. McCallum, Oxford 1946, p. 309.

32 *London and Westminster Review*, XXXII, 1838, pp. 241-60.

33 Sir Charles Lucas's introduction to his 1891 edition of Lewis, *Government of Dependencies*, p. xxvii.

34 Nicholas Mansergh, 'Some Reflections on the Transfer of Power in Plural Societies', in C. H. Philips and M. D. Wainwright, editors, *The Partition of India: Policies and Perspectives, 1935-1947*, London 1970, p. 44.

Lord Durham, the disclosures made and theories propounded by the very able men who accompanied him, raised in political thinkers a suspicion of the insecurity and injustice of colonial government by the mother country; and directed the thoughts of the more speculative towards the renewal of the older and freer polity of our first American settlements.'[35] The lack of an explicit reference to the Report of Lord Durham is testimony to the influence of Mill, for in *Representative Government* in 1859 he had attributed the Report to Wakefield and Buller.[36] When Merivale had lectured at Oxford in 1839, 1840 and 1841 he had not given any sign that the Report had aroused any sort of suspicions in his mind, nor does he seem to have referred to it in his years at the Colonial Office. In 1861 he made it clear that he was writing of a phase of imperial history which belonged to the past. Durham and the Colonial Reformers he regarded as 'bold and far-seeing innovators' but 'they miscalculated the means' of reaching their ends. 'They wished at once to give full municipal freedom to the colonists, and to tie down the land system of the colonies by strict regulation. The latter end of their commonwealth forgot the beginning.'[37]

Naturally it will be asked how the Report acquired such an undeserved position in Commonwealth history. Three main reasons may be advanced to explain the growth of the myth.

The principal reason was the apparent relevance of the Report to later imperial issues, and here the contradictions which had weakened the Report in 1839 served to make it universally acceptable. This process can be detected as early as Canadian Confederation. Here it may be argued that a wider measure of acceptance of the Report in the colonies began to filter back into British circles. In the eighteen-fifties colonial protagonists of British American Union made use of Durham's recommendation when they urged their schemes upon British statesmen.[38] In 1858 the *Morning Post*, in approving Sir Edmund Head's federal initiative, even quoted from the Report to prove that the colonies were like foreign states without diplomatic representation in their relations with each other.[39] When Confederation actually came

35 Herman Merivale, *Lectures in Colonization and Colonies delivered before the University of Oxford in 1839, 1840 & 1841*, London, 1861 ed., p. vi.

36 J. S. Mill, *Representative Government*, ed. R. B. McCallum, p. 309.

37 Herman Merivale, *Lectures*, 1861 ed., pp. vi-vii.

38 E.g. Public Record Office, CO 42/603, Anderson to Head, British Hotel, Ottawa City, Canada West, 24 January 1856, in Head to Labouchere, no. 20, Government House, Toronto, 30 January 1856, fos. 137-49. See also University of Nottingham, Newcastle Papers, NeC 9552, Francis Hincks to Colonel Bruce, Quebec, 18 December 1853. Hincks opposed union but regarded it as stemming from Durham's 'admirable report'.

39 *Morning Post*, 4 September 1858, and for quotation see C. P. Lucas, editor, *Lord Durham's Report*, II, p. 318.

into being, British ministers were concerned to demonstrate that it was not simply a .response to the American Civil War, or the outcome of Canadian political manoeuvrings. It had in fact been a widely accepted aim for many years past, and the point was most simply illustrated by reference to the Durham Report. A list of previous initiatives prepared in the Colonial Office and put into Confidential Print, began with the Report.[40] In introducing the British North America Bill into Parliament, Carnarvon in the Lords and Adderley in the Commons both began with similar references.[41] Neither quoted from the Report, although a sentence in Carnarvon's speech suggests he was familiar with it.[42]

These references to the Report can best be described as decorative or honorific. It was not central to the issue of Confederation and no-one suggested that it was. Nor had the position changed by the time of the Irish Home Rule controversy in 1886. Here was an issue – in many ways the touchstone of late nineteenth-century imperialism – which was centrally concerned with the relationship of a metropolitan and a dependent legislature, and one in which almost every conceivable precedent was considered, yet the Durham Report played only a minor part. In *England's Case against Home Rule* Dicey compared Home Rule with colonial independence, and in two essays in Bryce's *Hand Book* Thring referred extensively to colonial precedents.[43] Neither mentioned Durham, although Thring quoted from Burke and Merivale and specifically referred to the Canadian example.

The House of Commons debate on the second reading of the Home Rule Bill of 1886, a debate which lasted for twelve evenings, provides further illustration that the Report had acquired no more than a minor significance. The Canadian precedent was seen to be relevant to Ireland, but exactly how was not clearly established. Gladstone, in his opening speech, drew the parallel of Irish dissatisfaction and the Canadian rebellions of 1837, arguing the case that Canada did not win self-government because she was loyal and friendly, but became loyal and friendly as a result of a species of Home Rule.[44] John Redmond made the same point.[45] But on the sixth night a Unionist backbencher made

40 Public Record Office, CO 880/4, no. ix, fos. 63-8.
41 *Hansard's Parliamentary Debates*, 3rd series, CLXXXV, 19 February 1867, col. 557 (Carnarvon) and 28 February 1867, col. 1165 (Adderley).
42 Compare Carnarvon (*ibid.* col. 574): 'They stand to each other almost in the relation of foreign states', with C. P. Lucas, editor, *Lord Durham's Report*, II, p. 318.
43 A. V. Dicey, *England's Case against Home Rule*, London 1886, pp. 55-78, 194-213.
44 *Hansard's Parliamentary Debates*, 3rd series, CCCV, 10 May 1886, cols. 585-7.
45 *Ibid.* CCCV, 13 May 1886, cols. 966-8.

the telling point that the settlement of 1840 in Canada had failed because of the forced union of a Catholic and a Protestant population under one Parliament — from which it could be argued that to force Ulster to accept Dublin rule would be disastrous. 'It was the federation of the North American Colonies in the Dominion, and not the mere giving of responsible government to Canada, which proved a success'.[46] In his closing speech Gladstone cleverly turned the point, accepting that 'the stereotyped arrangements of the Union of 1840 were found to be totally inadequate' and implying that it was the creation of the provinces of Ontario and Quebec in 1867 which constituted the Home Rule precedent.[47] The Canadian precedent then was one which could be quoted by either side, and it was not in itself a decisive element in the debate. Moreover, these exchanges took place without any reference to the Durham Report. The omission is particularly striking in the case of Gladstone, who made three extended references to Canada in his speeches, reminding the House that 'in the early years of my Parliamentary life I took great interest in it, and some part in the great discussions on the disposal of Canada some fifty years ago'.[48] Twice he surveyed the history of Canada in detail. He referred also to the opposition he and Brougham had offered to the Rebellion Losses Bill of 1849, he referred to Russell's opinions on the relationship of Canada to Britain. At any of these points he might have mentioned the Durham mission or quoted from the Durham Report. He had lived through the events. He had read the Report within a week of its first appearance in 1839.[49] He was fighting to save his party and his ministry in one of the great political crises of the century, when every debating point might be worth a vote. Yet he made no use of the Durham Report.

Others did however, and the exchanges perhaps prove Gladstone was right to pass over it in silence. Childers, the Home Secretary, called Durham 'that far-seeing statesman' and offered a loose quotation from the Report, arguing that the Irish should be allowed to execute their laws as well as to make them.[50] Osborne Morgan, the Under-Secretary for Colonies, begged a number of questions with the assertion that Durham had 'recommended that Home Rule should be given to Canada'. He made play with the point that Canada, unlike Ireland, was

[46] *Ibid.* CCCVI, 25 May 1886, cols. 74-5 (by Westlake, MP for Romford).

[47] *Ibid.* CCCVI, 7 June 1886, cols. 1229-30.

[48] *Ibid.* Gladstone's references to Canada were on 10 May 1886, CCCV, cols. 585-7, and 7 June 1886, CCCVI, cols. 1223-4, 1229-30.

[49] M. R. D. Foot, *The Gladstone Diaries* (2 vols. continuing), Oxford 1968, II, pp. 580, 12 February 1839.

[50] *Hansard's Parliamentary Debates*, 3rd series, CCCV, 21 May 1886, cols. 1750-1: Compare Childers's quotation with C. P. Lucas, editor, *Lord Durham's Report*, II, p. 281.

thousands of miles away from Britain, and separated from the United
States 'by a hedge or a ditch, and in some parts merely by a parallel of
latitude'. Yet Canadian Home Rule had worked and, according to
Morgan, 'it was a remarkable fact that, in the very first Canadian Parliament which assembled under the Act, there sat the two gentlemen who
had headed the rebellion in Upper and Lower Canada, Mr. Mackenzie
and Mr. Papineau, both of whom became loyal subjects of the
Queen'.[51] It would indeed have been a remarkable fact had it been true.

Opponents of Home Rule argued that the Durham analogy was
irrelevant to Ireland.[52] Chamberlain refused to see the Report as a
single stroke of policy but as part of an evolutionary process. 'You will
have to give to Ireland all the reforms granted after Lord Durham's Act;
you will have to give them their practical independence, because there
is no use denying the fact, at this moment, the self-governing Colony of
Canada is practically independent.'[53] A more detailed reference to the
Report was made by Wodehouse, the MP for Bath. 'That famous State
Paper is a sort of landmark in Colonial history', he told the House. He
pointed out that Durham's recommendation of self-government was
intended for the English of Upper Canada, and that his intention was to
anglicise the French, a claim which he supported with extensive quotations from the Report. He concluded that 'this Canadian policy of
fusion and Legislative Union is the reverse of a precedent for an Irish
policy which despairs of fusion, and virtually destroys an existing Legislative Union'.[54]

The Report had not by 1886 become a particularly potent symbol.
It was referred to five times in the second reading debate, and quoted
twice, once by each side – as was *King Lear*. It was only one of a
number of colonial precedents alluded to in the debate,[55] and it is not
certain that any of them had much influence. Childers, with his welter
of examples, was followed by an Ulsterman who declared: 'I cannot
help thinking that the ultimate fate of this Bill will not be decided by
what Mr. Pitt said or did, or by what Sir Ralph Abercromby said or did,
but that it will be decided by the facts of the case as they exist in
1886.'[56] Certainly politicians displayed a more impressive grasp of the
facts of 1886 than of those of 1839. Inaccurate references to 'Lord
Durham's Act' and the miraculous conversion of Mackenzie and

---

51 *Ibid.* CCCVI, 4 June 1886, cols. 1035-6.
52 E.g. *ibid.* CCCV, 17 May 1886, col. 1191 (by King, MP for Hull Central).
53 *Ibid.* CCCVI, 1 June 1886, cols. 694-6.
54 *Ibid.* CCCVI, 3 June 1886, cols. 916-17. For quotations see C. P. Lucas, editor,
    Lord Durham's Report, II, pp. 288-307 various.
55 E.g. *Hansard's Parliamentary Debates*, 3rd series, CCCV, 13 May 1886, col.
    952; 18 May 1886, col. 1376; CCCVI, 4 June 1886, cols. 1064-70.
56 *Ibid.* CCCV, 21 May 1886, col. 1752 (Saunderson, MP for Armagh N.).

Papineau indicate that the Report was not a blueprint for action, but a vaguely identified and scarcely comprehended symbol, 'a sort of land-mark in Colonial History'.

The thirty years of controversy over Irish Home Rule legislation seems to have helped the growth of the Durham myth, particularly the notion of the continuing relevance of the Report. Even Sir Charles Lucas's scholarly introduction to his edition was not free from con-temporary polemics: his final chapter argued that Durham would have opposed Irish Home Rule.[57] The chapter was probably written as a riposte to Erskine Childers's attempt to cite the Report in support of the Irish cause.[58] Within twenty-four hours of the publication of the edition, this particular chapter had been taken up by *The Times*.[59] Scholarly reviewers regretted 'the intrusion of so topical a theme' in an academic work.[60] 'It is singular that a writer with the insight of Sir Charles Lucas should have allowed himself an indulgence in this little bit of contemporary political passion and prejudice, for the reference is out of place in such a work.'[61] Sixty years later it does indeed seem oddly out of place, but its inclusion becomes wholly intelligible when it is realised that even so great a scholar as Lucas saw the Report as a tract for the times.

If Ireland contributed to the revival of the Durham Report, it was South Africa which elevated it to mythological proportions. The parallels between the Canadian and South African situations were obvious, even if they did not run very deep. If men were influenced in their attitude to South Africa by the analogy of Canada, so too was their view of the Canadian experience coloured by its successor. The South African situation was one dominated by personalities, and this transmitted itself to the Canadian analogy. From one great high com-missioner men looked back to another, and Canada became increasingly synonymous with the Earl of Durham. 'If Sir Alfred Milner is to be the Lord Durham of South Africa, let us take care that the lesson from Lord Durham's failure be not forgotten.'[62] If Milner was to be the Durham of South Africa, Durham himself must naturally become 'Canada's celebrated proconsul'.[63]

57 C. P. Lucas, editor, *Lord Durham's Report*, I, pp. 318-24.
58 Erskine Childers, *The Framework of Home Rule*, London 1911, pp. 88-104.
59 *The Times*, 10 May 1912.
60 J. A. R. Marriott, 'The Evolution of Colonial Self-Government', *Fortnightly Review*, n.s. 92, 1 September 1912, pp. 393-409.
61 *Review of Historical Publications relating to Canada*, XVII, 1913, pp. 59-62.
62 *Spectator*, no. 3759, 14 July 1900, letter from 'X', 'Lord Durham and Canadian Reconstruction', pp. 36-7.
63 Violet R. Markham, 'Lord Durham and Canadian Self-Government', *Nine-teenth Century and After*, LIX, June 1906, pp. 914-23.

Men of all parties quickly discovered that in the Durham Report they had an inexhaustible supply of respectable quotations to justify their own wishes. Merriman publicly called for clemency to Cape Dutch who sided with the republics, arguing that Durham had shown clemency to the Canadian rebels, 'and the policy of Lord Durham in Canada was the real foundation of that British Empire of which we are so proud'.[64] The *Spectator* felt that Merriman wished to give the Boers a chance to win at the ballot box what they had lost in battle, and suggested that 'the Canadian precedent does not give too much help in detail, the cases being too dissimilar'. Even so, it made a bow in the direction of the man who was credited with the solution of that dissimilar problem. 'But though we cannot believe that Lord Durham would have approved such a policy, we are heartily at one with those who urge that the spirit in which Lord Durham approached the Canadian problem is the one in which the South African problem is to be approached.'[65] At the other extreme from Merriman, a Milnerite writing of the same political crisis in the Cape, in which responsible government broke down following a Bond boycott, could comment: 'The truth upon which Lord Durham insisted in his famous Report on Canada, that responsible government is only possible where an effective majority of the inhabitants are British, was once more demonstrated.'[66] If Liberals saw the Report as a magic conciliator, Conservatives saw it as a magic eradicator. One writer argued that Durham's French Canadian policy had been a success, and one which might be imitated – with Laurier seeming to be an imperialist and French Canadian troops on the Veld, it was hard to recall the true nature of Durham's wishes.[67] Garnett in 1902 insisted that the Report had been 'much misrepresented in England, and especially of late'. He felt obliged to deny that it was 'a complete surrender to the French Canadians, and framed with the sole motive of conciliating them'.[68]

In 1902 the Report was reissued by Methuen[69] – the first reissue since the Ridgway edition of 1839. Copies of the official Stationery Office edition of 1839 were 'not yet very scarce'[70] which is an interesting comment on public demand for the Report in the previous six

64 *Westminster Gazette*, 11 July 1900, statement by J. X. Merriman, Capetown, 20 June 1900, headed 'The Recent Crisis at the Cape'.
65 *Spectator*, no. 3759, 14 July 1900, pp. 36-7.
66 H. Basil Worsfold, *Lord Milner's Work in South Africa from its commencement in 1897 to the peace of Vereeniging in 1902*, London 1906, p. 480.
67 *Spectator*, no. 3759, 14 July 1900, p. 45.
68 R. Garnett, 'The Authorship of Lord Durham's Canada Report', *English Historical Review*, XVII, 1902, pp. 268-75.
69 *The Report of the Earl of Durham, Her Majesty's High Commissioner and Governor-General of British North America*, London 1902.
70 *Review of Historical Publications relating to Canada*, VII, 1903, pp. 53-4.

decades. 'The important questions of law and policy which the South African troubles have forced on the attention of the nation have naturally revived interest in the famous report in which, more than sixty years ago, Lord Durham discussed a somewhat similar situation in Canada. The report has been exhumed, reprinted, and made the subject of numerous essays describing it as, which it really is, a kind of Magna Charta or palladium of colonial freedom, and manual of the principles which should govern the relations between the mother country and her English-speaking dependencies.'[71] In 1906, Stuart Reid, Durham's first major biographer, explained that the reissue was prompted by the discussion of Milner's policy in South Africa.[72] The Durham Report was on the way to becoming an accepted symbol for both sides in politics. The Liberals could point to it as a text giving historical respectability to their inclination to gamble on self-government, while the Tories could retort that Durham's attitude to the French foreshadowed Milner's policy of anglicising the Boers. Thus the Report belatedly gained the bi-partisan acceptance as a symbol which it had so conspicuously failed to win for its recommendations in 1839.

The canonisation process was helped on its way by the appointment of the ninth Earl of Elgin as Colonial Secretary in 1905. The coincidence of an Elgin at the Colonial Office and a Grey as Governor-General of Canada did not escape notice,[73] and Durham was the keystone in this particular piece of imperial genealogy. Elgin himself was the grandson of Durham and the son of the Elgin who had introduced responsible government into Canada. His formative years were deeply affected by his mother's worship of her dead husband and dead father, and he evidently bracketed them together as men who had worked for a common end and sacrificed their lives to the Empire. He regarded both the Durham Report and Walrond's biography of his father as essential reading on the question of the Transvaal constitution, giving a copy of Walrond to his Under-Secretary, Winston Churchill, and requiring the West-Ridgeway Committee which went out to South Africa to read the Report — which it obligingly quoted in its own report. He discussed Durham's ideas in correspondence with Selborne, British High Commissioner in South Africa, and Elgin's application of them with Winston Churchill.[74] In winding up his speech in the House

71 R. Garnett, 'The Authorship of Lord Durham's Canada Report', p. 268.

72 Stuart J. Reid, *op. cit.* II, p. 312.

73 E.g. *Review of Historical Publications relating to Canada*, XI, 1907, pp. 88-92, which believed that the fourth Earl Grey was the grandson of the third Earl. See also Violet R. Markham, 'Lord Durham and Colonial Self-Government', p. 914.

74 Ronald Hyam, *Elgin and Churchill*, pp. 13, 58, 139, 146, 57-8. See also George M. Wrong, *The Earl of Elgin*, London 1905, p. v and photograph of the ninth Earl with his father in 1859, facing p. 214.

of Lords announcing his South African policy in February 1906 he ended by appealing to 'a more authorative source than any of my own' and quoted the Report's condemnation of representative and irresponsible government. 'Many years ago a similar question arose in another great colony, where the principles of responsible government were advocated and put into force by my grandfather and father. It is, I confess, an encouragement to me, in the views I have ventured to express to your Lordships, that I am following the principles they thus professed and which resulted in the prosperous, and great, and loyal Dominion of Canada.'[75] That Elgin could so telescope the ideas of his two relatives shows that the real issue of colonial self-government had long been settled, and that differences which had once been of crucial importance could be subordinated to the similarities discernible by hindsight.

Two Conservative reviewers were quick to pounce on Elgin's use of his family tradition. 'If the Government appeal to Lord Durham's Report, we shall be well-content', said the *Quarterly*, which showed by extensive quotation that Durham favoured anglicisation and deplored that colonial policy should be at the mercy of the sport of parties in Britain — which here meant the inconvenience of the Unionist election defeat. 'If the Government is to be guided by the Durham Report, let it be guided by the whole document, and by its spirit, not by an isolated paragraph.'[76] Violet Markham attacked a more general ignorance which led to misrepresentation of the Report, but it was clearly the Government she had in mind in her challenge to extreme supporters of Boer self-government. 'Having appealed to Caesar, are the latter willing to abide by Caesar's judgment, or only by such portions detached from the context, as may suit their own opinions?' Yet an examination of the extracts from the Report given by Miss Markham shows a cavalier attitude on her part to rendering Durham his due in accurate quotation.[77]

Similar exchanges took place in the Commons debates on South Africa. Lyttelton objected to the speed with which self-government was to be introduced into the Transvaal. 'In the great classic instance of

---

[75] *Hansard's Parliamentary Debates*, 4th series, CLII, 26 February 1906, cols. 748-9. For Elgin's quotations, see C. P. Lucas, editor, *Lord Durham's Report*, II, pp. 79-82 various.

[76] *Quarterly Review*, CCIV, June 1906, pp. 375-89, 'The Government and South Africa'.

[77] Violet R. Markham, *op. cit.* Her quotations are to be found variously in C. P. Lucas, editor, *Lord Durham's Report*, II, pp. 16, 60-1, 103, 192-3, 281-2, 282, 282-3 (these last three quotations include a linking half-sentence supplied by Miss Markham and passed off as Durham's own), 288-9, 296, 290 (these last two quotations form a composite).

Canada Lord Durham recommended the transition to be made deliberately "in order that a popular Government in which an English majority
shall permanently predominate" might be secured.' This quotation
from the Report was so strongly criticised by Dilke and Molteno, son of
the former Cape premier, that in the published volume of *Hansard*
Lyttelton wrote it out, replacing it with a reference to the fact that
Durham's recommendations were not carried out at once.[78] Molteno
paraded the standard Liberal quotations — that representative and
irresponsible government could not succeed, that the Crown must
choose its advisers from the majority, that the British public was un-
avoidably ignorant of the colonies.[79] Dilke on the other hand was the
one man who not only criticised the relevance of the Durham Report
but refused to subscribe to the myth at all. In July 1906 he seemed
unaware that Durham had written a Report, for he assumed that
Lyttelton was quoting from 'a speech of Lord Durham'. Durham's
French Canadian policy was, he said, 'such a hopeless example of
failure' that it could not be considered as a basis for policy in South
Africa.[80] In December 1906, when Churchill quoted Durham's 'conclusive authority' on the failure of representative government,[81] Dilke
attacked the Under-Secretary's 'amazing statement'. He could not see
the slightest evidence for the claim that representative and irresponsible
government could not be combined. 'The whole history of the Empire
contradicted that very rash assertion of Lord Durham.' Quite correctly
he pointed out that there had been colonies which had been governed
in that way for centuries.[82] Although Dilke seems to have been the only
man who openly challenged Durham's wisdom, his attitude illustrates
that the Report bore on only one aspect of the South African situation,
and was not necessarily a document of relevance to the wider issues of
the Empire. For Dilke, unlike most of his contemporaries, was interested not so much in white self-government as in African rights. Hence
he appealed, by implication, not to the Canadian situation but to the
West Indies. It was an indication that as imperial problems came to

---

[78] Compare the Parliamentary report of *The Times*, 1 August 1906, with
Hansard's Parliamentary Debates, 4th series, CLXII, 31 July 1906, col. 756.
Lyttelton's speech in *Hansard* is asterisked to show revision by its author.

[79] *Ibid.* col. 789, 792-3. Molteno's quotations are to be found in C. P. Lucas,
editor, *Lord Durham's Report*, II, 79-80, 103, 278, 263-4.

[80] *Hansard's Parliamentary Debates*, 4th series, CLXII, 31 July 1906, col. 766.

[81] *Ibid.* CLXVII, 17 December 1906, col. 1066. Churchill's quotation is in C. P.
Lucas, editor, *Lord Durham's Report*, II, pp. 79-80.

[82] *Hansard's Parliamentary Debates*, CLXVII, 17 December 1906, col. 1091. See
also the speech of Walker, MP for Melton, who referred to Durham's opinion
that representative government must fail, but called the eighth Earl of Elgin
'the real originator of self-government in Canada. . .' (cols. 1098-9).

involve wider questions of race relations than those of Boer and Briton in South Africa, and wider problems of colonial self-government than involved white Transvaalers, the Durham Report would cease to be a durable symbol.

Even at the height of the South African problem the Report was clearly a symbol and not a blueprint. Neither the Unionists nor the Liberals had a South African policy which was consistent with Durham's recommendations for Canada. The Liberals wanted self-government and a recognition of the identity of the Boer people. The Unionists wanted a policy of anglicisation combined with representative government. The similarities with the Durham Report were purely accidental, and each side appealed to it only where it supported their own views.[83] It had become 'a work which everybody quotes and some people read'.[84] Perhaps too it was a work which fewer people understood. It was certainly put to diverse uses by Elgin's colleagues in the Liberal government of 1905. Churchill, in a highly secret memorandum on South Africa, declared in 1906 that the Cabinet was 'absolutely determined to maintain, in the words of Lord Durham's Report, "a numerical majority of a loyal and English population"'. Campbell-Bannerman on the other hand insisted that 'Lord Durham did not try to make Frenchmen into Englishmen. He did not propose to . . . swamp them with new settlers. . .'. Ronald Hyam has understandably called this 'an unduly favourable interpretation' of the Durham Report.[85]

As important as the use of the Report in British politics was its position as the symbol of Canadian identity. The question of Canada's position in the Empire remained a current issue in Canadian politics down to 1931, affecting Canada's relations both with Britain and the United States. To both Canadians needed to prove that self-government and membership of the Empire were compatible. Here Durham made an ideal contemporary hero. A man who in himself reconciled the oppo-

---

83 See p. 50 above for Charles Buller's criticism of Pakington for citing only the parts of the Report he happened to agree with.

84 J. A. R. Marriott, 'The Evolution of Colonial Self-Government', p. 394.

85 Ronald Hyam, *op. cit.* pp. 140-1, 182-3. Churchill's quotation is in C. P. Lucas, editor, *Lord Durham's Report*, II, p. 299. It is interesting and perhaps alarming to note that just as the Edwardian liberals lauded the Report in proportion to their belief in the virtues of self-government, so in 1971 Professor Neale explicitly referred to the disillusionment felt in the nineteen-sixties with Parliamentary government, in criticising Durham for his belief in responsible government anchored to British institutions. Yet Durham's ideas were scarcely identical to the parliamentary system of a century later, and a criticism on these lines perversely contributes to the belief that the Report is of contemporary relevance. In fairness, it must be said that Professor Neale's comment is an aside. (R. S. Neale, 'Roebuck's Constitution and the Durham proposals', p. 581.)

sites of aristocracy and democracy, who preached with such confident prophecy the reconciliation of self-government and colonial status – such a man was the ideal symbol of Canadian identity. According to Chester New, Durham left Canada to write the Report 'more a Britisher than ever; through storm and pain he had served Britain all his life, but he served her best by becoming now – a Canadian'.[86] Not merely did the Durham symbol reconcile Canadian nationhood with the Empire, but it was also acceptable to the United States. He had after all been the first man since Lafayette to be invited to stay at the White House as the guest of the American people.[87] For better or worse, Canadian nationhood and the Durham Report became inextricably interwoven. The anonymous editor of the 1902 Methuen edition of the Report pictured Durham lying in his grave at Lambton. 'The western winds, blown from Canadian snows, visit his resting place, and, it may be, bear him tidings of the nation which his noble mercy and his wisdom made free and loyal.'[88]

According to tradition, Durham played his own part in this developing identification by his deathbed prediction: 'Canada will one day do justice to my memory.' Here was a great national task for Canada to undertake, an expression of its national status and an answer to its doubts. It is no accident that the Durham papers were one of the first major private collections to be acquired by the Public Archives of Canada, nor that Durham's principal biographer should have been Chester New, a Canadian. Whether Durham really did utter such a deathbed sentiment is difficult to know. It would have been curiously consistent if even in death there had to be public relations. What does seem likely is that he did not use the words the twentieth century has attributed to him. Dent in 1881, Garnett in 1898 and Bradshaw in 1903 quoted the tradition not as 'Canada will one day do justice to my memory' but as 'The Canadians will one day do justice to my memory'.[89] It was Stuart Reid in 1906 who made the substitution in the motto which appeared on the title-page of the second volume of his biography of Durham. The change is of some importance. 'The Canadians' in 1840 meant the people of two colonies in the St Lawrence valley. 'Canada' in 1906 was a transcontinental dominion. History was amended to serve contemporary needs. Stuart Reid showed

---

[86] Chester W. New, *op. cit.* p. 474.

[87] *Ibid.* p. 470.

[88] *The Report of the Earl of Durham*, p. xix.

[89] J. C. Dent, *op. cit.* I, p. 11; Richard Garnett, *Edward Gibbon Wakefield. The Colonization of South Australia and New Zealand*, London 1898, p. 183; F. Bradshaw, *Self-Government in Canada and how it was achieved: the story of Lord Durham's Report*, Westminster 1903, p. 256.

this clearly in the closing words of his biography: ' "Canada will one day do justice to my memory". Surely that day is at hand.'[90] Forty years later Sir Reginald Coupland took up the same theme. 'The prophecy has been fulfilled. The only first-rate biography of Durham has been written by a Canadian.'[91] Even Chester New, who kept that first-rate biography commendably free from non-historical comment, took the opportunity of his preface to say: 'Here I have only one confession to make. I am a Canadian of the third generation and all of my grandparents were living in Canada in Lord Durham's day. That subjects me, I feel confident, to no party bias, but it does expose me to a pride that in the life of my own country there have developed certain world-shaping conceptions.'

There could be no fairer nor more honest summing-up of the relationship between articulate Canadians of the first half of the twentieth century and the Durham myth. Even Chester New had originally intended 'to add an epilogue tracing those ideas from Lord Durham to their fulfilment in our own day, showing that it was our Canadian forefathers who cherished most warmly Durham's conceptions, that it was they who took the lead in insisting that the British Empire should not break up again, and in bringing his vision of the permanence and character of the Empire to a fuller fruition than even he had dreamed'. Here however loyalty to Clio triumphed over loyalty to Canada, and New 'decided that that was another story'.[92] But even in the mind of Durham's most scholarly biographer, doing justice to Durham's memory could not be separated from doing honour to his own country.

An event of symbolic importance may lose its relevance as circumstances change. Between the two world wars this process was going on both in Canada and in the Empire at large. Only two years after the publication of Chester New's biography, the passage of the Statute of Westminster effectively reduced the question of Canada's national status to a minor position, thus reducing the value of the Durham symbol. Indeed it would become a particularly unhelpful symbol of national identity once the implications of bi-culturalism had succeeded imperial relations as the central issue of Canadian nationhood. As there had been no place for the French in Durham's Canada, so there would be no place for Durham in modern Canada. But symbols do not disappear overnight. In 1939 the Report received the unique tribute of a centenary edition of the *Canadian Historical Review.*[93]

---

90 Stuart J. Reid, *op. cit.* II, p. 376.
91 R. Coupland, editor, *The Durham Report*, p. iii.
92 Chester W. New, *op. cit.* p. ix.
93 *Canadian Historical Review*, XX, June 1939.

In 1948 a French translation of the Report appeared, the first since the hasty newspaper productions of 1839.[94] The editor, Marcel-Pierre Hamel, offered an account of the Durham mission with particular emphasis on his relations with French Canada. In particular he pointed to the contrast between the high hopes with which the French received Durham and the bitter disillusion which followed.[95] For Durham, who arrived at Quebec as if he were a Byron coming to give his life for Canadian liberty, fell under the sway of men like Adam Thom, whose policy towards the French amounted to another St Bartholomew's massacre.[96] But this did not lead Hamel to challenge the belief that the Durham Report was the fount of subsequent Canadian history. On the contrary he accepted that Durham inspired the Union of the Canadas and the Confederation of 1867.[97] Indeed he went even further, suggesting that these two measures were but steps towards the creation of a transcontinental legislative union, designed to destroy the identity of French Canada. The Durham Report was still the blueprint of an Ottawa-led conspiracy to erode provincial autonomy, a Machiavellian plot to submerge Quebec in an Anglo-Saxon melting pot.[98] The Durham Report was still a relevant document but it had ceased to be a benevolent one.

In the Empire at large it was becoming increasingly irrelevant. By 1945 Sir Reginald Coupland could lament that 'outside Canada, few books so famous have been, in recent years at any rate, so little read'.[99] The early twentieth century had seen the Report as a Magna Carta of the colonies, from which the history of the Empire had flowed. The Balfour Report and the Statute of Westminster altered it to one of 'the great milestones'[100] on the road to the new Commonwealth. Durham,

---

94 M-P. Hamel, editor, *Le Rapport de Durham*, Quebec 1948.

95 *Ibid.* pp. 16-26.

96 Cf. *ibid.* p. 16 'évoquant déjà une espèce de Byron allant offrir sa vie à la liberté canadienne. . .' and the description of Thom, pp. 19-20, who 'ne prêchait ni plus ni moins qu'une Saint-Barthélémy de tous les Canadiens français'.

97 *Ibid.* p. 35: 'Il faut être aveugle, en effet, pour ne pas reconnaître que Durham a accompli de grandes choses. Il est à n'en pas douter l'inspirateur de l'Union de 1841, de la Confédération de 1867, de l'Union législative de demain, peut-être, si personne ne réagit contre le péril imminent.'

98 Of the Report: 'Il est l'arsenal où les hommes d'Etat canadiens vont puiser leur inspiration centralisatrice.' On assimilation: 'Machiavel n'aurait pas imaginé mort ni plus lente ni plus sûre.' 'La lecture de ce document peut engendrer du pessimisme sur l'avenir du Canada français. . . Mais ce n'est pas une raison pour le peuple canadien-français de démissioner. Nous ne serons jamais les assimilés de la Louisiane. Demain tout recommence' (*ibid.* pp. 50, 46, 50-1).

99 R. Coupland, *op. cit.* p. iii.

100 J. H. Thomas's phrase in 1931. *Hansard's Parliamentary Debates*, 5th series, Commons, CCLIX, 20 November 1931, cols. 1174-5.

the great radical who had formerly been praised for his single master-stroke of policy, was subtly transmuted from revolutionary to gradualist.[101] The Balfour Report was 'the normal and logical outcome of the Durham Report'.[102] When J. H. Thomas introduced the Statute of Westminster Bill into the House of Commons, he quoted Durham's insistence on the need to govern colonies through their own representatives, but stopped short of mentioning the four reservations. 'The Dominions having once started on the road there could be no halting place short of entire and complete autonomy.'[103] The only other speaker to refer to Durham was Leopold Amery, who also represented him as a believer in autonomy for colonies by instalments. He said that the Report had suggested 'the greater the responsibility you gave and the nearer the equality to this country, the closer would be their attachment to us and the greater the unity of the Empire'.[104] The four reservations had disappeared from sight.

The central problem of British imperial policy was no longer relations with self-governing white colonies but the challenge of nationalist India. To say that in relation to early twentieth century Canada and South Africa the Report had been a symbol is by no means to decry it. The Durham Report was at the height of its fame and of its influence in those years — although less for what it said than for what men thought it said. Unfortunately it failed utterly to translate to the Indian situation, and its utility as a symbol ceased. In 1886 the Report had been quoted in the Commons debates on Irish Home Rule. In 1906 it had grown to be a significant debating point in Parliamentary debates on South Africa, and it was still worth a mention in the Commons debate on the Statute of Westminster Bill in 1931. When the Indian Independence Bill came before the House of Commons in 1947, there was not one reference to the Durham Report. Yet throughout the debate there was a persistent note of congratulation, with references to the Commonwealth, to the fulfilment of mission, and the virtues of self-government.[105]

---

101 Professor Cell has recently pointed out how far Durham's approach to the Canadian problem can be seen in terms of the Utilitarian belief in all-embracing strokes of policy. In 1839 it seems unlikely that Durham intended his recommendations to be a step towards total autonomy. What he would have thought in 1926 or 1931 is a profitless speculation (J. W. Cell, *op. cit.* pp. 100-1).

102 V. Halperin, *Lord Milner and the Empire*, p. 222.

103 *Hansard's Parliamentary Debates*, 5th series, CCLIX, 20 November 1931, cols. 1174-5. For Thomas's quotations, see C. P. Lucas, editor, *Lord Durham's Report*, II, pp. 277-8 various. Thomas did not go on to quote from *ibid.* pp. 281-2.

104 *Hansard's Parliamentary Debates*, 5th series, Commons, CCLIX, 20 November 1931, col. 1199.

105 *Ibid.* CCCCLIX, 10 July 1947, cols. 2441-550.

The Durham Report could not be translated into Indian terms. In 1912 Sir Charles Lucas tried to apply Durham's ideas on a rule of thumb basis. Since India had neither an anglicised population nor formed a legislative union, he concluded to give responsible government would be to place the sub-continent 'in a category to which it does not naturally belong' with alien institutions which would be neither intelligible nor useful to the vast majority of Indians.[106] Professor Mansergh has told how a new recruit to the Colonial Office just after the second war was given a copy of the Durham Report to be read by an Under-Secretary who remarked: 'This is still essential reading for all of us.' Professor Mansergh adds: 'I doubt if this ever happened in the India Office.'[107] Such attempts as were made to apply the analogy were unproductive. Sir Reginald Coupland correctly guessed that the failure of Durham's four reservations made it likely that dyarchy could not be indefinitely continued[108] – a conclusion which could equally have been deduced from Indian reality. Less constructive was Coupland's use of Durham to argue against Partition, arguing that a bi-national state had been constructed in Canada despite the 'war of races'. Despite Durham's highly coloured account, French-English tensions in Canada were in no way comparable to the Hindu-Muslim hatreds in India.[109] This was recognised by a back-bench MP in 1947. 'The case of Canada is not an analogy at all. It is true that there were two races in Canada, in feud, the British and the French, but they shared a common European tradition.'[110] The most remarkable use of the Durham analogy in India was made not by a historian but by a politician. In February 1942 Attlee argued in favour of sending a senior minister to India to attempt to reach a settlement with Congress on a timetable for independence. 'There is a precedent for such action,' he wrote. 'Lord Durham saved Canada to the British Empire. We need a man to do in India what Durham did in Canada.'[111] The Cripps Mission which followed was a remarkable piece of historical parallel. Cripps – coincidentally the most radical politician of his day – could offer immediately only responsible

106 C. P. Lucas, *Greater Rome and Greater Britain*, pp. 149-50.
107 Nicholas Mansergh, 'Some Reflections on the Transfer of Power in Plural Societies', in C. H. Philips and M. D. Wainwright, *The Partition of India*, p. 44.
108 R. Coupland, *The Indian Problem 1833-1935*, Oxford 1942, pp. 39, 58.
109 R. Coupland, *The Future of India*, Oxford 1943, pp. 13-14.
110 *Hansard's Parliamentary Debates*, 5th series, CCCCXXXIX, Commons, 10 July 1947, cols. 2477-8. (Richards, MP for Wrexham.)
111 N. Mansergh and E. W. R. Lumby, editors, *Constitutional Relations between Britain and India: The Transfer of Power 1942-1947*, vol. I (London 1970), document no. 60, Memorandum by Attlee, 'The Indian Political Situation', 2 February 1942, pp. 110-12.

government limited by a large imperial factor. Like Durham, Cripps failed to secure the adoption of his plan and like Durham's it would probably have proved unworkable. 1947 was to show in India what 1847 had shown in North America — that formal imperial control could not be preserved where it was not accepted. Durham then had no place in India. Sir Reginald Coupland had to admit that 'the Canadian situation was not comparable with the Indian'. Professor Mansergh was more picturesque in his recollection of Morley's phrase that 'the fur coat of Canada was not suited to India's tropical clime'.[112]

The second reason for the growth of the Durham myth lies in the general revival of interest in the early Victorian empire builders which took place around 1900. Biographies and new fame were acquired by Durham, by Molesworth, by Roebuck, by Adderley and even by Wakefield.[113] It was a surprisingly uncritical process. Elgin, who admittedly had been the subject of one biography, did acquire a second, but Grey, perhaps the greatest of all mid nineteenth-century Colonial ministers, went unsung.[114] Sir James Stephen received no more than a privately produced eulogium by his daughter, who was more concerned to clear her father of suspicions of religious heterodoxy than to explain his contribution to the Empire.[115] John Morley even made an attempt — albeit unconvincing — to hoist Gladstone on to the colonial reform bandwaggon, although Gladstone's contribution had been at best minor and at worst — as in 1849 — obstructive.[116] The late Victorian and Edwardian biographers were extremely unselective in their subjects and concentrated to a disproportionate extent on minor figures. The men on whom the accolade of posterity was thus bestowed tended to have one element in common — all had been outsiders, critics of the govern-

---

112 R. Coupland, *The Indian Problem*, p. 19; Nicholas Mansergh, 'Some Reflections on the Transfer of Power in Plural Societies', in C. H. Philips and M. D. Wainwright, editors, *op. cit.* p. 45; and compare Lord Morley, *Indian Speeches (1907-1909)*, London 1909, pp. 35-6, speech at Arbroath, 21 October 1907.

113 Stuart J. Reid, *Life and Letters of the First Earl of Durham, 1792-1840* (2 vols.), London 1906; Millicent G. Fawcett, *Life of the Rt. Hon. Sir William Molesworth, Bart.*, London 1901; R. E. Leader, editor, *Life and Letters of John Arthur Roebuck, with chapters of autobiography*, London 1897; W. S. Childe-Pemberton, *Life of Lord Norton (Sir Charles Adderley) Statesman and Philanthropist*, London 1909; R. Garnett, *Edward Gibbon Wakefield: The Colonization of South Australia and New Zealand*, London 1898.

114 T. Walrond, editor, *Letters and Journals of James, Eighth Earl of Elgin*, London 1872; George M. Wrong, *The Earl of Elgin*, London 1905.

115 Caroline E. Stephen, *Sir James Stephen: Letters with biographical notes by his daughter*, Gloucester, private, 1906.

116 John Morley, *op. cit.*, I, book iii, ch. iii, 'Party Evolution — New Colonial Policy', pp. 351-65.

ments and policies of their day. One generation repudiated the ortho-
doxies of its predecessor, forgave Wakefield his seductions and Durham
his arrogance as they indiscriminately threw out the good with the bad.

The biographical process was to some extent self-generating. Lives of
Wakefield and Elgin touched on Durham.[117] The 1902 reissue of the
Report was followed by a book on the Canadian mission[118] and then by
a major biography which had been long in preparation.[119] This in turn
paved the way for the Lucas edition of 1912. Such publications gave
rise both to general essays and to learned reviews and articles.[120]
Severally they constituted the conventional wisdom which fed the
Durham myth. H. E. Egerton was one man who believed that this
should be exactly the function of any biographer of Durham. Stuart
Reid insisted that the Canadian mission should not be allowed to over-
shadow Durham's earlier career.[121] Egerton disagreed. 'Lord Durham's
claim to eminence in general rests on his Canada report; and therefore
the first volume of this biography . . . deals with details on a scale out
of proportion with the present importance of the subject.'[122]

There is a good deal of evidence that the Edwardians were conscious
that they were reviving and not continuing the memory of Durham. A
correspondent of the *Spectator* in 1900 welcomed Merriman's statement that Durham had laid the foundation of British imperial policy. 'I

---

117 R. Garnett, *Edward Gibbon Wakefield*, pp. 176-83; George M. Wrong, *The
Earl of Elgin*, pp. 20-38.
118 F. Bradshaw, *Self-Government in Canada and how it was achieved: the story
of Lord Durham's Report*, Westminster 1903.
119 Stuart J. Reid, *op. cit.* I, p. vii.
120 The following periodical articles deal in part with Durham: *Quarterly Review*,
CLXXXVII, January 1898, 'Colonial Champions in the Mother Country', pp.
153-76; *Quarterly Review*, CCIV, April 1906, 'The Government and South
Africa', pp. 375-89; Violet R. Markham, 'Lord Durham and Colonial Self-
Government', *Nineteenth Century and After*, LIX, June 1906, pp. 914-23;
Edinburgh Review, CCV, January 1907, 'The First Earl of Durham and
Colonial Aspiration', pp. 246-72; H. Bruce Dodwell, 'The First Earl of
Durham', *Macmillan's Magazine*, n.s. II, April 1907, pp. 547-60; S. J.
McLean, 'Canadian Problems and Parties', *Quarterly Review*, CCIX, July
1908, pp. 168-93; J. A. R. Marriott, 'The Evolution of Colonial Self-
Government', *Fortnightly Review*, n.s. XCII, 1 September 1912, pp.
393-409. The main academic article on Durham was R. Garnett's 'The
Authorship of Lord Durham's Canada Report', *English Historical Review*,
XVIII, 1902, pp. 268-75, with reply by Hugh E. Egerton, *ibid.* p. 539. For
academic reviews, see *English Historical Review*, XVIII, 1903, pp. 825-6 (by
Egerton), *ibid.* XXII, 1907, pp. 187-8 (by Egerton), *ibid.* XXVII, 1912, pp.
796-7 (by W. L. Grant); *Review of Historical Publications relating to Canada*,
VII, 1903, pp. 53-4, *ibid.* VIII, 1904, pp. 30-3, *ibid.* XI, 1907, pp. 88-92,
ibid. XVII, 1913, pp. 59-62.
121 Stuart J. Reid, *op. cit.* I, p. ix.
122 *English Historical Review*, XXII, 1907, pp. 187-8.

should like to know why this is so seldom recognised, and why Lord Durham's name and reputation have been so unjustly treated by so many writers?'[123] Garnett in 1902 spoke of a revival of interest in the Report which had been 'exhumed' and reprinted.[124] Reid in 1906 placed Durham's recovery in the immediate past. 'The reputation of no public man in England in the Nineteenth Century has suffered more undeserved neglect than that of Lord Durham; indeed, until recent years saw the nation confronted in South Africa, with a similar problem to that which he solved in Canada in 1838-9, it was the fashion to ignore the splendid achievements of his public career.'[125] It was certainly difficult to understand how Reid's could be the first biography if Durham had enjoyed such fame for so long. 'That the *Life* of a leader so conspicuous should not be written until nearly seventy years after his death is indeed singular; that it should have been written at all, in spite of such a lapse of time, is a tribute to the enduring character of Lord Durham's fame.'[126] Such comments could only be made internally consistent by speaking of a renewed rather than a continuing fame. By the time of the Lucas edition in 1912 the battle for recognition was won. 'Lord Durham is certainly coming to his own as a maker of history.'[127] 'Lord Durham's Report may be said to have attained to the dignity of a classic.'[128]

The Edwardians who perceived that they were witnessing and assisting in a revival were correct. Durham had died in 1840. No reissue of the Report appeared until 1902. No book about him was published until 1903. The *Quarterly Review* issued decadal indexes, which contained detailed references to subjects referred to in articles, and were not simply lists of titles. From these it may be said with confidence that no mention of the Earl of Durham was made in its pages between 1841 and 1898 — the former unfavourable, the latter laudatory.[129] The revival may also be traced in the literary career of Stuart Reid. Durham had appeared in his two previous biographies of early Victorians, Sydney Smith in 1884 and Russell in 1895. Reid was a discursive

---

123 *Spectator*, no. 3760, 21 July 1900, pp. 79-80. The letter was from T. H. Lambton. Efforts to trace a relationship with the Durham family have not been successful. Merriman's letter was in *Westminster Gazette*, 11 July 1900.
124 R. Garnett, 'The Authorship of Lord Durham's Canada Report', p. 268.
125 Stuart J. Reid, *op. cit.* I, p. viii.
126 *Review of Historical Publications relating to Canada*, XI, 1907, p. 89.
127 *Review of Historical Publications relating to Canada*, XVII, 1913, p. 59.
128 J. A. R. Marriott, 'The Evolution of Colonial Self-Government', p. 394.
129 *Quarterly Review*, CXVII, March 1841, pp. 477-80 and *ibid.* CLXXXVII, January 1898, pp. 168-71. The index volumes consulted were vols. LXXX, 1850, C, 1858, CXXI, 1867, CXL, 1876, CLX, 1885, CLXXXI, 1895, CCI, 1905. These index volumes covered the years 1837-1904.

writer, yet in his life of Smith he said nothing of Durham's services to the Empire. In 1895 he referred to 'the greatness and far-reaching nature of his services' to the Crown and Canada, but without allusion to the Report – and this despite a brief discussion of Russell's time at the Colonial Office.[130]

This upsurge of interest in the early Victorian empire-builders is itself a phenomenon requiring explanation. There was of course a wider reading public, the generation made literate by the Education Act of 1870. But the growth of the elementary schools hardly explains the enthusiasm of Egerton and Lucas, or the reappearance of Durham in the *Quarterly Review*. The Durham revival was part of a more complex process of late Victorian imperialism, which with its increased emphasis on martial values was inclined to the cult of the hero. One indication of this was a revival of interest in Carlyle's *On Heroes*[131] – a work first published in 1841. The late Victorian Empire was not over-generously supplied with heroes, and needed to manufacture them in retrospect. A public which could lionise Milner, Rhodes, Jameson, Seddon and the memory of Gordon was evidently not over-critical. The heroes who were re-discovered from the past were seen in terms of their contemporary counterparts. Thus Durham owed part of his celebrity to Milner, while Molesworth, a radical imperialist, was consciously equated with Chamberlain.[132]

Of all the early Victorian figures, Durham was the most likely to win for himself a lasting place in the pantheon. He possessed two undeniable advantages. The first was that the climax of his life lent itself to romantic drama. If to the picture of a man sacrificing himself to the Empire could be added the sub-plot of the hero struggling in vain to put forward the truth and the nation realising its error just too late to do him honour, then there would be an uplifting and almost unchallengeable theme for any biographer. 'About to die, he was to render her [i.e. England] the service which stands peerless in Imperial history. His Report was more than a work of genius; his whole conduct in the coming months was more than that of a man of state. He wrought his miracles for ages to come, not only through his superior intellectual gifts, but because he set behind him all personal ambitions and all personal feelings, conquered temper and pride – dogging him through

---

130 Stuart J. Reid, *A Sketch of the Life and Times of Sydney Smith*, London 1884; Reid, *Lord John Russell*, London 1895, esp. pp. 110-11, 116-22.

131 Thomas Carlyle, *On Heroes, Hero-Worship and the heroic in history*, first published 1841. Of twenty-seven editions in the British Museum catalogue (1965) in the English language, twenty-one were published between 1888 and 1912. For Carlyle's notion of how colonies should be governed, see C. A. Bodelsen, *Studies in Mid-Victorian Imperialism*, London 1924, p. 31.

132 H. E. Egerton, editor, *Selected Speeches*, p. xi.

life, but subdued in that last great task.'[133] A dramatic life ends in tragic but grand catharsis, the hero becomes a demigod. There was a double duty to venerate this man, both for his contribution to imperial policy and to make good the injustice done to him in his own lifetime. Durham secured his place in the imperial pantheon not so much by his Report as by his death. He was a Milner, but with a dash of General Gordon, a Byron in prose. For the Report was the second advantage his memory possessed. It was undeniably a readable document, and it was easy to assume that what was readable was also influential. It is significant that a year after the reissue of the Durham Report, an edition of Molesworth's speeches appeared:[134] they too were readable and they too were without much influence on contemporaries. The confusion between readability and significance was best exploded by John Beverley Robinson in 1839. 'No one will deny to this very important state paper the merit of being ably written; but in respect to a document intended to affect such great interests, the style is but a secondary consideration.'[135]

It is in the men who have written about the Report that the third reason for Durham's reputation should be sought. Mill, Egerton, Lucas, Keith, Coupland and Mansergh — all wrote as constitutionalists, in the very best and highest sense. Lucas and Egerton were pioneers both in their rediscovery of the Report and — the latter even more than the former — in their tenacious defence of it.[136] They believed in the rule of the law, and hence in the force of the written word. Sir Reginald Coupland not only edited an edition of the Report, but produced a reflective three volume unofficial Report of his own on India.[137] To such men it was natural that history should be a catalogue not of crimes

133 Chester W. New, *op. cit.* pp. 473-4.
134 H. E. Egerton, editor, *Selected Speeches of Sir William Molesworth, Bart., P.C., M.P., on questions relating to colonial policy*, London 1903.
135 Public Record Office, CO 880/1, Confidential Print North America, no. 19, Robinson to Normanby, Spring Gardens' Hotel, 23 February 1839, fos. 237-42.
136 E.g. G. C. Lewis, *An Essay on the Government of Dependencies*, ed. C. P. Lucas, London 1891, esp. pp. 299n-300n; H. E. Egerton, *A Short History of British Colonial Policy*, London 1897, pp. 300, 304. See also Hugh E. Egerton, 'Lord Durham's Canada Report', *English Historical Review*, XVII, 1902, p. 539, a remarkably forceful rejection of Garnett's theory of multiple authorship of the Report although Garnett could cite the received tradition in his support. Other statements by Egerton which contributed to the Durham myth were at *ibid.* XVIII, 1903, pp. 825-6; *ibid.* XXII, 1907, pp. 187-8 and H. E. Egerton, editor, *Selected Speeches*, p. ix.
137 Coupland's three volumes — *The Indian Problem 1833-1935, Indian Politics 1936-1942*, and *The Future of India* were published at Oxford in 1942-3 as parts of 'a report on the constitutional problems of India submitted to the

and follies but of declarations and statutes. As believers in the ration-
ality and perfectability of political man, they were the imperial Whig
historians. In this it was natural that they should look to a great revelation from which flowed inevitably a Commonwealth of self-governing
nations. The Durham Report supplied the place of that revelation, and
it even had to be assimilated into the larger Whig tradition as 'the
Magna Carta of the Second British Empire'.[138] Sir Charles Lucas made
the most unequivocal and unself-conscious statement of this view in
1912: 'If England continues to be inspired by what Lord Durham
taught so well, then as Great Britain has grown into Greater Britain, so
Greater Britain will grow into greatest Britain, to the glory of God the
Creator, and the well-being of mankind.'[139]

It is clear then that an attack on the Durham Report is by implication an assault on a whole school of Commonwealth constitutional
history. To reject this approach is by no means to despise the spirit
behind it. It has contributed most of what has been humane in the
imperial experience and nearly all that is still alive in the Commonwealth today. But while the evolution of the Commonwealth cannot be
understood without an appreciation of this spirit, it by no means
follows that Commonwealth history should be viewed solely through it.
In that case, some alternative sketch of interpretation, however brief,
should be attempted. Perhaps it may be best to turn to the parallel
which so much attracted the men of Empire themselves — that of the
unification of Germany, which was brought about not by resolutions
and majorities but by iron and blood. The same elements may be seen
at work in imperial history. Iron and blood will embrace British indus-
trial might and the vast outpouring of migrants as well as the simple
element of military force which underpinned them. But force, as
Bismarck almost certainly knew, was important not so much in itself as
in the mystique of invincibility it created, the effect it could exercise
on men's minds. Here too is the place of the constitutional tradition
symbolised in Durham. Just as German unity in fact owed a great deal
to the resolutions and majorities which shared the idea in the minds of
men, so the imperial experience owed much to the Whig tradition,
which did something to soften its force and to give it the ethical and
religious sanction hymned by Sir Charles Lucas. Indeed so confused did
the martial themes of Empire become with the liberal notions of

Warden and Fellows of Nuffield College, Oxford' (title-pages). It is difficult
to avoid the belief that Coupland's approach was inspired by Durham,
especially since he produced his own edition of the Durham Report in 1945.

[138] The *Quarterly Review*, CLXXXVII, pp. 168-71, called it 'the Magna Carta
of colonial independence' in 1898.

[139] C. P. Lucas, editor, *Lord Durham's Report*, I, p. 317.

Commonwealth that the British people were able to make a remarkably painless transition from the one to the other, largely without realising the extent of their act of abdication. The historical explanation which will best dispel that confusion will be the one which interprets the history of the Empire-Commonwealth less in terms of the brilliance of Durham's prose and more in terms of the variations of British power. With conviction, if also with regret, an interpretation of Commonwealth history is offered here which owes more to Bismarck than to Durham.

Bibliography

A. DOCUMENTS

i. *Unpublished*

Aberystwyth, National Library of Wales, Harpton Court Collection.

Cambridge, University Library, Graham Papers (microfilm), Diary of Sir James Stephen.

Durham, Department of Palaeography and Diplomatic, University of Durham, Grey Papers.

Edinburgh, National Library of Scotland, Ellice Papers.

London, British Museum, Gladstone Papers.
    Peel Papers.

London, Public Record Office, Colonial Office series, CO 42/283, 284, 296-9, 310-11, 509, 518, 534, 536, 551, 558, 603, 614; CO 188/141: CO 537/137, 141-2; CO 880/1, 4.
    Ellenborough Papers.
    Russell Papers.

Nottingham, University Library, Newcastle Papers.

Ottawa, Public Archives of Canada, Derby papers (microfilm).
    Elgin Papers (microfilm).

ii. *Published*

    (a) *Official*

Parliamentary Papers, 1828, VII, 569, pp. 375-730 (Report of the Parliamentary Committee).

    1837, XXIV, 50, pp. 1-408 (Report of the Gosford Commission).

    1837, XLII, 0.42, pp. 1-4 (Russell's Ten Resolutions).

    1839, XXXII, 2, pp. 1-690 (Durham Report and despatches).

Hansard's Parliamentary Debates, 2nd to 5th series.

    (b) *Editions of the Report*

Coupland, R., editor, *The Durham Report, an abridged version with an introduction and notes*, Oxford 1945.

Craig, G. M., editor, *An abridgement of the Report on the Affairs of British North America by Lord Durham*, Toronto 1963.

Lucas, C. P., editor, *Lord Durham's Report on the Affairs of British North America* (3 vols.), Oxford 1912. Volume I is by Lucas, II and III are his edited version of the Report and appendices.

The Report and Despatches of the Earl of Durham. Her Majesty's High Commissioner and Governor-General of British North America, London 1839, published by Ridgway.

The Report of the Earl of Durham, Her Majesty's High Commissioner and Governor-General of British North America, London 1902, published by Methuen.

There is also a French edition edited by M-P. Hamel, *Le Rapport de Durham*, Quebec 1948.

(c) *Other printed sources*

Benson, A. C. and Lord Esher, editors, *The Letters of Queen Victoria: a Selection from Her Majesty's Correspondence between the years 1837 and 1861* (3 vols.), London 1907.

Broughton, Lord, *Recollections of a Long Life* (6 vols.), London 1909-11.

Brymner, Douglas, *Report on Canadian Archives for 1884*, Ottawa 1885.

Doughty, Arthur G., *Report on the Public Archives for the Year 1923*, Ottawa 1924.

Doughty, Arthur G., editor, *The Elgin-Grey Papers* (4 vols.), Ottawa 1937.

Egerton, H. E., editor, *Selected Speeches of Sir William Molesworth, Bart., P.C., M.P. on questions relating to colonial policy*, London 1903.

Egerton, H. E. and W. L. Grant, *Canadian Constitutional Development shown by selected speeches and despatches, with introductions and explanatory notes*, London 1907.

Esher, Lord, editor, *The Girlhood of Queen Victoria, A Selection from Her Majesty's Diaries between the years 1832 and 1840* (2 vols.), London 1912.

Foot, M. R. D., editor, *The Gladstone Diaries* (2 vols.), Oxford 1968.

Kennedy, W. P. M., editor, *Statutes, Treaties and Documents of the Canadian Constitution 1713-1929*, second edition, Oxford 1930.

Knaplund, Paul, editor, *Letters from Lord Sydenham Governor-General of Canada, 1839 to 1841, to Lord John Russell*, London 1931.

Lewis, Gilbert F., editor, *Letters of the Right Hon. Sir George Cornewall Lewis, Bart. to various friends*, London 1870.

Manning, William R., editor, *Diplomatic Correspondence of the United States: Canadian Relations 1784-1860* (4 vols.), Washington 1940-5.

Morley, Lord, *Indian Speeches (1907-1909)*, London 1909.

(Reeve, Henry, editor), *A Journal of the Reign of Queen Victoria from 1837 to 1852 (The Greville Memoirs)* (3 vols.), London 1885.

Sanders, Lloyd C., editor, *Lord Melbourne's Papers*, London 1889.

Selections from Speeches of Earl Russell 1817 to 1841 and from Despatches 1859 to 1865 (2 vols.), London 1870.

(d) *Newspapers and periodicals*

Courier 1840.
Daily News 1858.
Examiner 1838-40.
Globe 1838-9.
Leeds Mercury 1839-40.
Manchester Guardian 1839-40.
Metropolitan Conservative Journal 1839.
Morning Chronicle 1837-40, 1842, 1849.
Morning Herald 1838-9.
Morning Post 1837-9, 1858.
Spectator 1838-40, 1848, 1900.
Standard 1838-9.
Sun 1838.
The Times 1837-40, 1849, 1912.
Westminster Gazette 1900.
Canadian, British American and West Indian Magazine 1839.
Colonial Gazette 1840.
Colonial Magazine 1840, 1849.
Dublin Review 1839.
Dublin University Magazine 1839.
Eclectic Review 1839.
Edinburgh Review 1839, 1907.
Fortnightly Review 1912.
London and Westminster Review 1838.
Macmillan's Magazine 1907.
Monthly Review 1839.
Nineteenth Century and After 1906.
Quarterly Review 1839, 1841, 1898, 1906, 1908.
In addition other periodicals were searched, and mention should be made of the detailed index to the *Quarterly Review* from 1837 onwards.

B. SECONDARY WORKS

i. *Books*

Bagehot, Walter, *The English Constitution*, edited by R. H. S. Crossman, London 1963.

Bliss, Henry, *An Essay on the Re-Construction of Her Majesty's Government in Canada*, London 1839.

Bodelsen, C. A., *Studies in Mid-Victorian Imperialism*, London 1924.

Bradshaw, F., *Self-Government in Canada and how it was achieved: the story of Lord Durham's Report*, Westminster 1903.

Bryce, James, *The American Commonwealth* (3 vols.), London 1888.

Bryce, James, editor, *Hand Book of Irish Home Rule*, London 1887.

(Buller, Charles), *Responsible Government for Colonies*, London 1840, reprinted in E. M. Wrong, editor, *Charles Buller and Responsible Government*, Oxford 1926.

Bury, Viscount, *Exodus of the Western Nations* (2 vols.), London 1865.

Carlyle, Thomas, *On Heroes, Hero-Worship and the heroic in history*, London 1841.

Cell, John W., *British Colonial Administration in the Mid-Nineteenth Century: The Policy-Making Process*, London 1970.

Childe-Pemberton, W. S., *Life of Lord Norton (Sir Charles Adderley) Statesman and Philanthropist*, London 1909.

Childers, Erskine, *The Framework of Home Rule*, London 1911.

Chittick, V. L. O., *Thomas Chandler Haliburton ('Sam Slick') A Study in Provincial Toryism*, New York 1924.

Coupland, R., *The Indian Problem, 1833-1935*, Oxford 1942.
  Indian Politics 1936-1942, Oxford 1943.
  The Future of India, Oxford 1943.

Dent, J. C., *The Last Forty Years: Canada since the Union of 1841* (2 vols.), Toronto 1881.

Dicey, A. V., *England's Case against Home Rule*, London 1886.

Egerton, H. E., *A Short History of British Colonial Policy*, London 1897.

Facts Versus Lord Durham. Remarks on that portion of the Earl of Durham's Report, relating to Prince Edward Island, London 1839.

Fawcett, Millicent G., *Life of the Rt. Hon. Sir William Molesworth, Bart.*, London 1901.

Garnett, R., *Edward Gibbon Wakefield: The Colonization of South Australia and New Zealand*, London 1898.

Glazebrook, G. P. de T., *Sir Charles Bagot in Canada: a study in British Colonial Government*, Oxford 1929.

Gourlay, Robert, *General Introduction to Statistical Account of Upper Canada compiled with a view to a grand system of Emigration in connexion with a reform of the Poor Laws*, London 1822.

Grey, Earl, *The Colonial Policy of Lord John Russell's Administration* (2 vols.), London 1853.
  Parliamentary Government considered with reference to Reform, London 1864 edition.

(Haliburton, T. C.), *The Bubbles of Canada. By the author of 'The Clockmaker'*, London 1839.

(Haliburton, T. C.), *A Reply to the Report of the Earl of Durham. By a Colonist*, London 1839.

Halperin, V., *Lord Milner and the Empire. The Evolution of British Imperialism*, London 1952.

Head, Francis B., *A Narrative*, London 1839, third edition.

Horton, Robert Wilmot, *Ireland and Canada: supported by Local Evidence*, London 1839.

Huttenback, R. A., *The British Imperial Experience*, New York 1966.

Hyam, Ronald, *Elgin and Churchill at the Colonial Office 1905-1908: the watershed of the Empire-Commonwealth*, London 1968.

Kerr, D. G. G., *Sir Edmund Head: A Scholarly Governor*, Toronto 1954.

Leader, R. E., editor, *Life and Letters of John Arthur Roebuck, with chapters of autobiography*, London 1898.

Lewis, George Cornewall, *An Essay on the Government of Dependencies*, London 1841.

An Essay on the Government of Dependencies, edited by C. P. Lucas, Oxford 1891.

An Essay on the Influence of Authority in matters of opinion, London 1849.

Lucas, C. P., *Greater Rome and Greater Britain*, Oxford 1912.

Mansergh, Nicholas, *The Commonwealth Experience*, London 1969.

Mansergh, N. and E. W. R. Lumby, editors, *Constitutional Relations between Britain and India: The transfer of power 1942-1947*, first volume, London 1970.

Marryat, Captain, *A Diary in America with remarks on its institutions*, Part Second (3 vols.), London 1849-50.

Martineau, Harriet, *The History of England during the Thirty Years Peace 1816-1846* (2 vols.), London 1849-50.

McIntyre, W. D., *Colonies into Commonwealth*, London 1966.

McNaught, Kenneth, *The Pelican History of Canada*, Harmondsworth 1969.

Merivale, H., *Lectures on Colonization and Colonies delivered before the University of Oxford in 1839, 1840 and 1841* (2 vols.), London 1841-2, Second edition 1861.

Mill, J. S., *On Liberty and considerations on Representative Government*, edited by R. B. McCallum, Oxford 1946.

Morley, J., *Life of William Ewart Gladstone* (3 vols.), London 1903.

Murray, C. A., *Travels in North America during the years 1834, 1835 and 1836* (2 vols.), London 1839.

New, Chester W., *Lord Durham: A Biography of John George Lambton First Earl of Durham*, Oxford 1929.

Reid, Stuart J., *Life and Letters of the First Earl of Durham, 1792-1840* (2 vols.), London 1906.

Lord John Russell, London 1895.

A Sketch of the Life and Times of Sydney Smith, London 1884.

Richardson, Major, *Eight Years in Canada*, New York 1967, facsimile of 1847 edition.

Roebuck, J. A., *The Colonies of England: a plan for the government of some portion of our colonial possessions*, London 1849.

Ryerson, Egerton, *Sir Charles Metcalfe defended against the attacks of his late counsellors*, Toronto 1844.

Sharpe, L. L., *The Viceroy's Dream, or the Canadian Government not 'wide awake', A mono-dramatico-political poem*, London 1838.

Should Lord Durham be impeached? The question considered in an appeal to the electors of the House of Commons, London 1839.

Stephen, Caroline E., *Sir James Stephen: Letters with biographical notes by his daughter*, Gloucester (privately printed) 1906.

Tocqueville, Alexis de, *Democracy in America* (translated by Henry Reeve) (4 vols.), London 1835-40.

[Wakefield, E. G.], *A View of Sir Charles Metcalfe's Government of Canada*, London 1844.

[Wakefield, E. G.], *A View of the Art of Colonization*, London 1849.

Walrond, T., editor, *Letters and Journals of James, Eighth Earl of Elgin: Governor of Jamaica, Governor-General of Canada, Envoy to China, Viceroy of India*, London 1872.

Worsfold, H. Basil, *Lord Milner's Work in South Africa from its commencement in 1897 to the peace of Vereeniging in 1902*, London 1906.

Wrong, E. M., editor, *Charles Buller and Responsible Government*, Oxford 1926.

Wrong, George M., *The Earl of Elgin*, London 1905.

ii. *Articles*

Arbuthnot, Alexander, 'James Bruce, Eighth Earl of Elgin, *Dictionary of National Biography*, III, pp. 103-6.

Buller, Charles, 'Sketch of Lord Durham's Mission to Canada in 1838', in C. P. Lucas, editor, *Lord Durham's Report on the Affairs of British North America*, III, pp. 336-80.

Carr, William, 'Henry George Grey, Third Earl Grey', *Dictionary of National Biography*, Supplement II, pp. 361-4.

Conacher, J. B., 'Peel and the Peelites 1846-1850', *English Historical Review*, LXXIII, 1958, pp. 431-52.

Dobie, Edith, 'The Dismissal of Lord Glenelg from the office of Colonial Secretary', *Canadian Historical Review*, XXIII, 1942, pp. 280-5.

Egerton, Hugh E., 'Lord Durham's Canada Report', *English Historical Review*, XVII, 1902, p. 539.

Fryer, C. E., 'Lower Canada (1815-1837)', *Cambridge History of the British Empire*, VI, pp. 234-50.

Fox, Grace, 'The Reception of Lord Durham's Report in the English Press', *Canadian Historical Review*, XVI, 1935, pp. 276-88.

Gallagher, J. and R. Robinson, 'The Imperialism of Free Trade', *Economic History Review*, 2nd series, VI, 1953, pp. 1-15.

Garnett, R., 'The Authorship of Lord Durham's Canada Report', *English Historical Review*, XVII, 1902, pp. 187-98.

Hamilton, J. A., 'Edward Ellice', *Dictionary of National Biography*, XVII, pp. 246-7.

'Constantine Henry Phipps, First Marquess of Normanby', *ibid.* XLV, pp. 230-1.

Irving, T. H., 'The Idea of Responsible Government in New South Wales before 1856', *Historical Studies Australia and New Zealand*, XI, 1963-5, pp. 192-205.

Lowenthal, David, 'The Maine Press and the Aroostook War', *Canadian Historical Review*, XXXII, 1951, pp. 315-36.

MacNutt, W. S., 'New Brunswick's Age of Harmony: the Administration of Sir John Harvey', *ibid.* pp. 105-25.

Mansergh, Nicholas, 'Some Reflections on the Transfer of Power in Plural Societies', in C. H. Philips and M. D. Wainwright, editors, *The Partition of India: Policies and Perspectives 1935-1947*, London 1970, pp. 43-53.

Martin, Chester, 'Sir Edmund Head's First Project of Federation, 1851', *Canadian Historical Association Annual Report for 1928*, pp. 14-26.

    'Sir Edmund Head and Canadian Confederation, 1851-1858', *Canadian Historical Association Annual Report for 1929*, pp. 5-14.

Morison, J. L., 'The Mission of the Earl of Durham', *Cambridge History of the British Empire*, VI, pp. 289-307.

Neale, R. S., 'Roebuck's Constitution and the Durham Proposals', *Historical Studies Australia and New Zealand*, XIV, April 1971.

iii. *Reviews*

Burroughs, Peter, review of Chester New's *Lord Durham* in *Canadian Historical Review*, LII, 1971, pp. 190-1.

Egerton, H. E., review of Bradshaw's *Self-Government in Canada* in *English Historical Review*, XVIII, 1903, pp. 825-6.

    Review of Reid's *First Earl of Durham*, in *ibid.* XXII, 1907, pp. 187-8.

Grant, W. L., review of C. P. Lucas, editor, *Lord Durham's Report* in *ibid.* XXVII, 1912, pp. 796-7.

Review of Historical Publications relating to Canada, VII, 1903, pp. 53-4; VIII, 1904, pp. 30-3; XI, 1907, pp. 88-92; XVII, 1913, pp. 59-62.

Smith, William, review of New's *Lord Durham* in *Canadian Historical Review*, XI, 1930, pp. 49-53.

Biographical Notes

Adderley, Charles Bowyer, first Baron Norton (1814-1905). Conservative politician. Under-Secretary for Colonies 1866-8. Enthusiastic, popular and incompetent.

Amery, Leopold Stennett (1873-1955). Conservative politician. Colonial Secretary 1924-9, Dominions Secretary 1925-9.

Attlee, Clement Richard, first Earl (1883-1967). Labour politician. Deputy Prime-Minister 1940-5. Prime Minister 1945-51.

Bagot, Sir Charles (1781-1843). After a diplomatic career, in which he negotiated the Rush-Bagot Treaty of 1817 by which Britain and the USA agreed not to arm on the Great Lakes, he became Governor-General of Canada in 1842. Soon after his arrival Lord Sydenham's coalition ministry lost its majority in the Assembly, and Bagot was forced to admit French and Reform leaders to government.

Baldwin, Robert (1804-58) and his father, William Warren (1775-1844). Moderate reformers who developed theories of responsible government. Robert Baldwin held office briefly in 1836 and again with LaFontaine in 1842-3 and from 1848-51. One of the greatest figures in Canadian history.

Balfour, Arthur James, first Earl of Balfour (1848-1930). Conservative politician. Prime Minister 1902-5. Sat in Conservative Cabinets until 1929 as elder statesman. Presided over Balfour Report of 1926 on the structure of the Commonwealth.

Brougham, Henry Peter, first Baron Brougham and Vaux (1778-1868). Lord Chancellor 1830-4. A leading Whig, law reformer and intriguer. He quarrelled with Durham in 1834.

Bryce, James, first Viscount Bryce (1838-1922), historian, jurist, Liberal politician.

Buller, Charles (1806-48). A popular radical, MP 1832-48. Secretary to Durham in 1838. One of the most likeable and least shady characters in the Durham entourage.

Campbell-Bannerman, Sir Henry (1836-1908). Liberal Prime Minister 1905-8.

Carnarvon, fourth Earl of (Henry Howard Molyneux Herbert, 1831-90). Conservative politician. Under-Secretary for Colonies 1858-9, Colonial Secretary 1866-7, 1874-8.

Cathcart, Charles Murray, second Earl Cathcart (1783-1859). Soldier. Commander-in-chief in Canada 1845-7. Appointed Governor-General during the war scare over American claims in Oregon.

Chamberlain, Joseph (1836-1914). Radical turned Liberal Unionist when he opposed Irish Home Rule in 1886. Colonial Secretary 1895-1903. Believer in closer Imperial unity.

Childers, Erskine (1870-1922). Irish Nationalist. Author of *The Riddle of the Sands*. Shot in 1922.

Childers, Hugh (1827-96). Liberal politician. 1851-7 lived in Australia. Held office in various Liberal ministries from 1865 to 1886.

Churchill, Sir Winston (1874-1965). Began his ministerial career as Under-Secretary for Colonies 1905-8. Prime Minister 1940-5, 1951-5.

Colborne, Sir John, first Baron Seaton (1778-1863). Soldier. Lieutenant-Governor of Upper Canada 1829-36, but remained in Canada as commander-in-chief and put down the rebellions of 1837-8. Acting Governor-General before Durham arrived and after he left.

Coupland, Sir Reginald (1884-1952). Fellow of All Souls College Oxford 1920. Member of the Cripps Mission to India 1942. Edited Durham Report 1945.

Dilke, Sir Charles Wentworth (1843-1911). Liberal politician, with an interest in the Empire. His career was wrecked by a divorce case.

Durham, first Earl of (John George Lambton, 1792-1840). Whig politician. MP 1813, Baron 1828, Earl 1833. Lord Privy Seal 1830-3, and earned the nickname 'Radical Jack' for his part in drawing up the Reform Act of 1832. Ambassador Extraordinary to St Petersburg, 1832, 1835-7. High Commissioner in Canada 1838. Author of the Durham Report 1839.

Egerton, Hugh Edward (1855-1927). Fellow of All Souls College Oxford and Beit Professor of Colonial History 1905-20.

Elgin, eighth Earl of (James Bruce, 1811-63). Governor of Jamaica 1842-6, after a short period as a Conservative MP. Governor-General of Canada 1847-54, where he introduced responsible government. His second wife, Lady Mary Lambton, was Durham's daughter. Elgin subsequently conducted two missions to China, sat in the Cabinet and went out to govern India, where he died.

Elgin, ninth Earl of (Victor Alexander Bruce, 1849-1917). Liberal politician. Grandson of Durham, and born in Canada while his father was Governor-General. Colonial Secretary 1905-8.

Ellenborough, first Earl of (Edward Law, 1790-1871). Conservative politician, mainly interested in India.

Ellice, Edward, the elder (1791-1863). Whig politician and party manager. Held office 1832-4 but preferred to work behind the scenes. Extensive land and fur trading interests in Canada. Known as the 'Bear'. His son, Edward Ellice the younger (1810-80) accompanied Durham to Canada in 1838 and was captured in the rebellion.

Galt, Sir Alexander Tilloch (1817-93). Canadian Finance Minister 1858-62, when he vindicated Canada's right to control her own tariffs.

Gipps, Sir George (1791-1847). Commissioner in Canada 1835-7. Governor of New South Wales 1838-46.

Gladstone, William Ewart (1809-98). Began his ministerial career as Under-Secretary for Colonies in a Conservative government in 1834-5. Colonial Secretary 1845-6. Took a general, if unsympathetic interest in Canadian affairs at this period. Later, as a Liberal, he decided he had been wrong about Canada and decided to do better in Ireland. Prime Minister 1868-74, 1880-5, 1886, 1892-4.

Glenelg, first Baron (Charles Grant, 1778-1866). Whig politician. Fellow of Magdalene College, Cambridge 1802. Colonial Secretary 1835-9. Likeable but inept.

Gordon, Charles George 'Chinese' (1833-85). Soldier. His adventures in various parts of the world ended with his death at Khartoum.

Gosford, Archibald, second Earl of (1776-1849). Leader of a three-man commission of enquiry in Canada while Governor-General 1835-7.

Gourlay, Robert Fleming (1778-1863). Radical. Early projector of British North American Union. Forced to leave Canada in 1819 by 'Family Compact' Tories.

Graham, Sir James Robert George (1792-1861). Colleague of Durham in drawing the Reform Bill. Left the Whigs with Stanley in 1834 and became close friend of Peel.

Greville, Charles Cavendish Fulke (1794-1865). Diarist and gossip.

Grey, Sir Charles Edward (1785-1865). Commissioner in Canada 1835-7. West Indian Governor 1841-53.

Grey, Charles, second Earl (1764-1845). Whig politician. Prime Minister 1830-4, and carried the Reform Act. Of his many children, his daughter Louisa married Durham.

Grey, Henry George, third Earl (1802-94). Known as Lord Howick 1807-45. Whig politician. His liberal views on Canada were occasionally heeded by his colleagues in the eighteen-thirties. As Earl Grey he was Colonial Secretary 1846-52 and carried his ideas into practice.

Haliburton, Thomas Chandler (1796-1865). A Nova Scotian Tory whose comic novels about 'Sam Slick' made him popular in England.

Harvey, Sir John (1778-1852). Soldier and colonial governor in New Brunswick 1837-41, Newfoundland 1841-6, and Nova Scotia 1846-52. Although his over-enthusiastic handling of the Maine boundary dispute in 1839 weakened the case for responsible government, he presided over its first introduction to a colony in 1847.

Head, Sir Edmund (1805-68). Lieutenant-governor of New Brunswick 1848-54, and Governor-General of Canada 1854-61. A scholar interested in federal government.

Head, Sir Francis Bond (1793-1875). Lieutenant-governor of Upper Canada 1835-8. Best described as mildly eccentric. Distant cousin of Sir Edmund Head.

Hobhouse, John Cam, first Baron Broughton (1786-1869). Whig politician and diarist.

Howe, Joseph (1804-73). Nova Scotian Reformer. His immense energy was not always matched by his judgement. Early advocate of responsible government.

Howick, Lord, *see* Grey, Henry George.

Jameson, Sir Leander Starr (1853-1917). Conservative politician in Cape Colony. His inept raid on the Transvaal in 1895 made him a minor imperial hero.

Labouchere, Henry, first Baron Taunton (1798-1869). Whig politician. Under-Secretary for Colonies 1839, Colonial Secretary 1855-8.

LaFontaine, Sir Louis Hyppolyte (1807-64). Moderate Reform leader of French Canada. In office 1842, 1848-51.

Lewis, George Cornewall (1806-63). Whig politician and intellectual who wrote on colonial government. Friend of Sir Edmund Head.

Lucas, Sir Charles Prestwood (1853-1931). Head of the Dominions Department of the Colonial Office 1907-11. Published a number of books on colonial history, including the most complete edition of the Durham Report in 1912.

Lyttelton, Alfred (1857-1913). Liberal Unionist politician and cricketer. Colonial Secretary 1903-5.

Lytton, Sir Edward George Earle Lytton (1803-73), changed name to Bulwer Lytton in 1843; became Baron Lytton 1866. Novelist, friend of Durham. Radical politician who turned Conservative in 1852. Colonial Secretary 1858-9.

Mackenzie, William Lyon (1795-1861). Upper Canada Reformer who led the rebellion of 1837.

MacNab, Sir Allan Napier (1798-1862). Upper Canada Tory.

Melbourne, second Viscount (William Lamb, 1779-1848). Whig politician. Prime Minister 1834, 1835-41. Both in his style of political leadership and in his private life he harked back to the eighteenth century.

Merivale, Herman (1806-74). Professor of Political Economy at Oxford 1837-42, where he lectured on colonial government. Permanent Under-Secretary at the Colonial Office 1848-59.

Merriman, John Xavier (1841-1926). Liberal politician in Cape Colony.

Metcalfe, Sir Charles Theophilus, first Baron (1785-1846). Governor-General of Canada, 1843-5 after a career spent in India and Jamaica. Quarrelled with Reformers over his insistence on an independent executive role.

Mill, John Stuart (1806-73). Philosopher and Utilitarian. Associate of Wakefield and supporter of Durham.

Milner, Sir Alfred, first Viscount (1854-1925). High Commissioner in South Africa 1897-1905. Played no small part in causing the South African War, and wished to extinguish the Dutch language and identity.

Molesworth, Sir William (1810-55). Radical baronet who took a spasmodic interest in colonial reform.

Molteno, Percy Alport (1861-1937). Liberal MP 1906-14. Son of J. C. Molteno, first Premier of Cape Colony.

Morley, John, first Viscount (1838-1923). Liberal politician. Secretary of State for India 1905-10. Biographer of Gladstone.

Mulgrave, *see* Normanby.

Neilson, John (1776-1848). Leading English speaking Reformer in Lower Canada.

New, Chester William (1882-1960). Historian and Professor at McMaster University. Biographer of Durham (1929).

Newcastle, fifth Duke of (Henry Pelham Fiennes Pelham, 1811-64). Colonial Secretary 1853-4, 1859-64.

Normanby, first Marquis of (Constantine Henry Phipps, 1793-1863). Governor of Jamaica 1832-4, Lord Lieutenant of Ireland 1835-9. Colonial Secretary, February to August 1839. His son, Lord Mulgrave (George Augustus Constantine Phipps, second Marquis, 1819-90) was an army officer in Canada in 1838 and served as lieutenant-governor of Nova Scotia 1858-63.

O'Connell, Daniel (1775-1847). Leader of Irish Catholics in Parliament. Campaigned for Repeal of the Union of 1800 but never earned his nickname 'the Liberator'.

Pakington, Sir John Somerset, first Baron Hampton (1799-1800). Conservative politician, MP 1837-74. Colonial Secretary. Of limited ability.

Papineau, Louis Joseph (1786-1871). Lower Canada Radical who became an implacable enemy of the British connection. Implicated in the 1837 rebellion but fled to the USA.

Peel, Sir Robert (1788-1850). Conservative leader who broke his party by accepting Free Trade in 1846. Prime Minister 1834-5, 1841-6.

Redmond, John Edward (1856-1918). Irish Nationalist, who succeeded Parnell as party leader in 1890. Political mission to the Irish in the colonies 1882-4. A moderate.

Reid, Stuart J. (d. 1927). Author of many biographies, including the first major life of Durham (1906).

Rhodes, Cecil John (1853-1902). Defies political classification. An Imperialist who emigrated to South Africa in 1880 and became a diamond millionaire. His flamboyant schemes to extend British rule in Africa resulted in the annexation of Rhodesia.

Robinson, Sir John Beverley (1791-1863). Upper Canada Tory and an able intriguer. Chief Justice of Upper Canada from 1830.

Roebuck, John Arthur (1801-79). Radical politician. Agent for Lower Canadian Assembly. Except in Canadian affairs a Jingo before his time.

Russell, Lord John, first Earl (1792-1878). Whig-Liberal politician. MP 1813. Main influence on the Reform Bill of 1832, and virtually deputy leader of the Whigs under Melbourne. Colonial Secretary 1839-41, 1855. Prime Minister 1846-52, 1865-6. Although grandfather of Bertrand Russell, he did not always display the same power of logical thought.

Ryerson, Egerton (1803-82). Leader of the Canadian Methodists.

Seaton, Lord, *see* Colborne.

Seddon, Richard John (1845-1906). Liberal politician in New Zealand, where he was known as 'King Dick'. A great success with the British public during the Jubilee of 1897.

Selborne, second Earl of (William Waldegrave Palmer, 1859-1942). Liberal Unionist politician. Cabinet minister 1900-5. Governor of the Transvaal and High Commissioner in South Africa 1905-10.

Smith, Sydney (1771-1845). Whig, clergyman and wit.

Spring Rice, Thomas, first Baron Monteagle (1790-1866). Whig politician. Chancellor of the Exchequer 1835-9.

Stanley, Edward George Geoffrey Smith (1799-1869). Known as Lord Stanley 1834-51, when he became fourteenth Earl of Derby. Broke with the Whigs over the Irish Church issue in 1834, became a Conservative but broke with Peel over Free Trade in 1846. Colonial Secretary, 1833-4, 1841-5. Prime Minister, 1852, 1858-9, 1866-8.

Stephen, Sir James (1789-1859). Permanent Under-Secretary at the Colonial office, 1836-47. An Evangelical of great ability. His reserved manner made him unjustifiably disliked.

Stuart, Sir James (1780-1853). Lower Canada Tory, suspended from office in 1830 because of suspicion of corruption. Lobbied for union of the provinces in 1822 and from 1837. Durham made him Chief Justice of the court of Queen's Bench at Montreal.

Sydenham, first Baron (Charles Poulett Thomson, 1799-1841). Whig politician and cabinet minister 1834, 1835-9. Governor-General of Canada 1839-41. The Union was carried through under his masterful influence.

Tocqueville, Alexis de (1805-59). French writer on political institutions.

Thom, Adam (1802-90). Editor of the *Montreal Herald*, and author of *Anti-Gallic Letters*, 1836. One of Durham's advisers.

Thomas, James Henry (1874-1949). Labour politician. Colonial Secretary 1924, 1931, 1935-6. Dominions Secretary 1930-5.

Wakefield, Edward Gibbon (1796-1862). Colonization theorist and controversialist. Imprisoned in Newgate for abduction 1826-9. Although disguised in economic terms, his theories were really designed to create a stratified society in the colonies.

Index